Praise for *The Seeker and The Teacher of Light*

"*The Seeker and the Teacher of Light* presents a compelling and exciting story about the nature of reality and our place in it. Combining the work of truly pioneering scientists, modern-day philosophers and renowned healers, Dr. Gin brings to light the fundamental geometric structure embedded in all matter and shows us how to engage with and use those geometries for healing and growth. The teachings of Joachim Wippich add an exhilarating and empowering dimension to the scientific information in this book. By synthesizing cutting-edge scientific research with a deep, evolutionary spirituality, Dr. Gin helps us to expand the context within which we see ourselves. As we embrace a larger view of ourselves and our place in the cosmos, we can learn to draw on our innate capabilities to bring harmony and balance to ourselves and our world. Part memoir, part scientific thesis, and part spiritual text, this unique book offers an intriguing look at our evolving understanding of the world and invites us to make a giant leap forward."

—JUDY KITT, President, Foundation for Mind Being Research (FMBR)

"As I read your text, I feel a true and sincere heartfelt passion to share what you have learned and what has unfolded throughout your life. Because of your personal experiences and your true passion, I feel your book will touch many people's hearts and allow them to experience, for themselves, who they really are and what they have come to do in this lifetime. I also feel this book is not only timely but also a great practical handbook and reminder for self-realization because of where humanity finds itself today—faced with the quandary of fully embracing its higher evolutionary path. Well done, my friend."

—CAROLINE CORY, Executive Producer, Documentary Film & Digital Media: *www.SuperhumanFilm.com*

"I have known Jerry for many years as a kind, generous, and open-minded seeker. He has been sincerely exploring healing and spirituality to enhance his life's journey, and has shared his discoveries and learnings in his book."

—MADA ELIZA DALIAN, author of *In Search of the Miraculous: Healing into Consciousness,* and creator of the Dalian Method

"Dr. Jerry Gin offers a pathway towards evolving consciousness, and successfully unites the scientific and spiritual communities. Learn how the work of scientists like Nikola Tesla, Marcel Vogel, and Walter Russell supply foundational support for the profound I AM affirmations of Master Dowser and Spiritual Teacher Joachim Wippich. Understanding the essence of I AM is a key step for achieving harmony and balance."

—JAN WALSH, IFSG and BG-EHS Practitioner

"An urgent message for humanity is pouring in from many directions — we are beings of consciousness temporarily inhabiting bodies. The message is: 'Wake up! Grow in awareness of the subtle energies around us.' Dr. Gin's book clarifies the message, makes it coherent and accessible, and exciting.

"This book is a journey with a genius. In a heartfelt way he invites readers not only to understand, but also to have a direct experience through the techniques and exercises he offers. He convinces us that 'we all have the ability to affect the nature of matter' through practices such as pendulums and sacred number series.

"In the mid 1950s, another genius named Pierre Teilhard de Chardin, a French Jesuit priest and also a scientist, wrote about the Omega Point. He predicted that there would come a time of coalescence, when the advances of science and the essence of spirituality would be integrated into a unified field of understanding of the physical world and the dimensions that lie beyond. Dr. Gin's life has been, and continues to be, an exploration of that integration. As guide and fellow seeker, he shares with us the insights he's gained so far."

—CYNTHIA SPRING, co-author of channeled books, *Seven Questions about Life After Life*, and *Seven Questions about the Greater Reality*

"This is a wonderful book. The content is accessible, flows well, reads easily, and I was hooked right from the start. This feels like a gift because it is perfectly aligned with my own journey of believing in our innate abilities to awaken to a higher consciousness."

—JANE MAJKIEWICZ, editor, *writeintuition.com*

"*The Seeker and the Teacher of Light* takes us on a journey to understand the being of our essence — the spark of life that begins even before we are a physical body. By understanding our essence, we can heal ourselves through bringing ourselves into harmony, into the Consciousness — the Oneness — of I AM.

"Dr. Gin offers insight into the healer's various tools, bringing in science as well as the healing modalities of eastern spirituality, dowsers, mystics, and mediums. Gin explains the reason for the success of the healings, which are both biological and spiritual: True healing is achieved through non-judgment, compassion, forgiveness, and love.

"Woven throughout the book are Affirmations by healer Joachim Wippich (the Teacher of Light referred to in the title) to raise our level of Consciousness through balance and harmony, by introducing us to the healing wisdom of the I AM. Through these affirmations, we come closer to understanding ourselves, our essence, compassion, and love."

—REGINA OCHOA, Channeler, Medium

"*The Seeker and the Teacher of Light* has infused my spiritual understanding with a level of intelligence and optimism for which I am exceedingly grateful. Bringing a scientific mind together with a seeker's openness, Dr. Gin explores the nature of the universe with passion and precision, and brings his own findings — as well as the healing contributions of his mentor, Joachim Wippich — down to earth (so to speak) in applicable ways.

"So we are offered, on one end of the spectrum, the immensity of the universe and its ongoing creation to ponder; and on the other end, very practical ways of aligning ourselves with the highest vibration, the 'I AM,' the essence of each one of us reading this book. You can make a pendulum (recipe included) or buy one, and with it find out what you are in resonance with — what's good for you and what isn't. You can lift the energy in a room . . . in a bodily cell that's out of harmony . . . your thoughts. All you need is to be open to the premise of the book — that we are spirits in a body — and try out the offerings here. Wippich's unique affirmations, in particular, can give you the experience of who you are when not weighed down by limiting ideas and self-concepts. Take this book into your life, and notice the lift in your spirit — and an increased awareness of being connected to all of life."

—NAOMI ROSE, author, *Starting Your Book: A Guide to Navigating the Blank Page by Listening to What's Inside You*

The Seeker and The Teacher of Light

*On the Teachings of Joachim Wippich
and the Mystery of 3-6-9*

JERRY GIN

Torus Press

The Seeker and the Teacher of Light: On the Teachings of Joachim Wippich and the Mystery of 3-6-9, by Jerry Gin. Copyright © 2021 by Jerry Gin. All rights reserved.

No part of this publication may be reproduced, distributed, or transmitted in any form or by any means, including photocopying, recording, or other electronic or mechanical methods, without the prior written permission of the publisher, except in the case of brief quotations embodied in critical reviews and certain other noncommercial uses permitted by copyright law. For permission requests, write to the publisher, addressed "Attention: Permissions Coordinator," at the address below:

Torus Press
www.jerrygin.com
Email: *jerry@jerrygin.com*

Cover illustration:
Mary Lou Arum / *mlaaccess@hotmail.com*

Developmental Editor / Editor / Publishing Coordinator:
Naomi Rose / *www.naomirose.net*

Typesetting and Design:
Margaret Copeland, Terragrafix / *www.terragrafix.com*

Proofreading:
Gabriel Steinfeld / *www.gabrielsteinfeld.com*

Printed in the United States of America
First printing 2021
ISBN# 978-1-7363982-0-3

Dedication

This book is dedicated to the light that is Joachim Wippich. His deep insight as to the nature of harmony and understanding our true I AM nature has driven me to write about this information. The knowledge is too important for humanity not to know about, and needs to be presented.

To bring in the energy of Harmony for yourself and for this book...

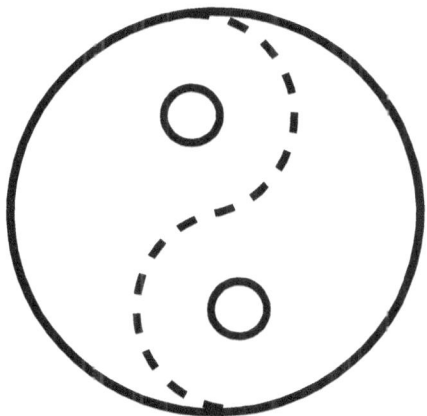

With a pen or pencil, draw over the dotted line of the yin yang symbol, above, in one continuous motion. The Harmony energy will appear when the line is drawn.

In the final chapter on 3-6-9 energies (Chapter 13), you will learn how to detect the Harmony energy.

At the end of that chapter, there will be another yin yang structure with the dotted line within the yin yang symbol, where the dotted line has not been filled in and there is no Harmony energy. You can then compare the energy of that structure with the above structure, which has the Harmony energy.

Fill in the space below with your Full Birth Name, and you are on your way to learning about your true essence.

I AM _____
       (Full Birth Name)

Table of Contents

Introduction	xvii
CHAPTER 1. Journey from Bending Spoons and Dowsing to Healing, and My Friend Joachim	1
Meeting Joachim Wippich	3
Spreading Joachim's Teachings	4
CHAPTER 2. Joachim's Central Message about Healing and Remembrance	5
CHAPTER 3. You Are Not Just Your Body	7
What Quantum Physics Tells Us	9
The Brain: What It Is (and Isn't)	10
The Cleve Backster Experiments	12
Conscious Intention	14
Energies Surrounding a Person	14
Innate Abilities	18
Death Is Just a Journey to Another Level of Vibration	23
CHAPTER 4. As Above, So Below — The Formation of Matter	29
The Vortex Motion of Light, and Creation	29
What Brings About Harmony and Disharmony	31
Walter Russell's View of Creation	32
A Clairvoyant Understanding of the Atom	40
The Torus Structure	40
CHAPTER 5. How We Create from Our Thoughts	47
Creating a Desired Reality	49
CHAPTER 6. I AM	53
I AM Links Us to Our True Nature as God's Thought Creation	54
There Is No Intermediary between You and God	54
CHAPTER 7. Harmony and Balance	61
Achieving Health, Happiness, and Harmony	61
Polarity Seeks Balance	62
The Principle of Balance/Harmony	64
Joachim's Way of Bringing in Harmony	65
CHAPTER 8. Dowsing, Harmony, and the Vibrational Level	67
Our Vibrational Level	67
Dowsing Works with the Subconscious	68

Dowsing to Determine Your Vibrational Level	69
Mental Dowsing vs. Vibrational Dowsing (Radiesthesia)	70
Standard, or Mental, Dowsing	71
Using a Pendulum for Mental Dowsing	72
Vibrational Dowsing, or Radiesthesia	77
Using a Neutral Pendulum for Vibratory Dowsing (Radiesthesia)	80
The Neutral Pendulum and Your Personal Wavelength	82
Viewing Your Vibrational Level	86
Putting Yourself into Harmony	88
Raising Your Vibrational Level	89

CHAPTER 9. Harmony and BioGeometry — 93

Detecting Subtle Energies for Locating Temples, Cathedrals… and More	93
BioGeometry and BG3	94
A Refresher on Resonance	95
The Amazing Results of Bringing in Harmony through Increased BG3	97
Using BioGeometry Tools to Understand Our Role as Creators	99

CHAPTER 10. Healing — Harmony and the Self (I AM) — 103

Joachim's Message on Harmony and Healing	104
Joachim on the I AM	105
Polarities Seek Harmony/Balance at the Center	106
Marcel Vogel: Lessons in Healing	107
Inviting Harmony into What Needs Healing	108
Harmony, BioGeometry, and Healing	109

CHAPTER 11. Joachim Wippich — Teacher of Light — 115

Joachim's Background	115
Joachim's Entry into Dowsing	116
Helping People Heal Themselves	117
Pearls of Wisdom from Joachim Wippich	119
Some Affirmations by Joachim Wippich	129
Table of Affirmations	129
Harmonic Dowsing	130
Harmony for Mother Earth	132
Affirmation for Healing the Planet	133
Harmony for the Physical Body	133
An Alternative Harmony Affirmation for the Physical Body	133
Harmony for the Immune System	134

Knowledge within Cellular Thoughts	134
Self-Correct When Not Feeling Well	134
Memory or Immune System	135
Harmonizing My Memory	141
A Healing Affirmation	141
For Harmonizing Breath and Regeneration	141
Rethink	141
Affirmation to Increase Your Vibrational Level (Useful for Dowsers)	142
Alternative Harmony and Raising Vibrational Level to the I AM	143
Knowledge	144
Spiritual Evolution 1	145
Spiritual Evolution 2	145
Getting a Good Night's Sleep	146
CHAPTER 12. Journey of a Seeker	**149**
My Early Years	149
My Business Years in the Science Field	153
My Spiritual Journey	157
CHAPTER 13. The Mystery of 3-6-9	**183**
3-6-9: The Key to the Universe	183
Key Religious and Ancient Spiritual Symbols and Structures Resonate with BG3	185
Instruction on Drawing the Torus to Show BG3	186
The Numbers 3-6-9	187
The Yin Yang Symbol	189
AUM in Sanskrit	191
The Math of the Torus	192
Bagua	194
Reiki Symbol of Power	195
BG3 Is Different from 3-6-9	196
Location of 3-6-9 and BG3 Resonant-Energy Qualities in Torus Structures	199
The Spiritual Aspect of 3-6-9	200
The Healing Aspect of 3-6-9	200
Conclusion	**203**
References: Text	205
References: Figures	213

Acknowledgments 217
About the Author 219

List of Figures

Figure 1. My first pendulum (a string and a nut), and some spoons turned into pretzels	2
Figure 2. The double-slit experiment	10
Figure 3. Kirlian photo of a dusty miller leaf	16
Figure 4. Model of a torus	30
Figure 5. Walter Russell's view of creation	34
Figure 6. The basis of the creation of matter	37
Figure 7. The basis of the creation of matter: the cones of the vortex	38
Figure 8. The basis of the creation of matter: Nature's method of storing energy in mass	39
Figure 9. The "Anu"—the basic building block of matter—the spiral motion of the aether	40
Figure 10. Vector Equilibrium (VE), or cuboctahedron	42
Figure 11. Cuboctahedron—Icosahedron—Octahedron	43
Figure 12. Isotropic Vector Matrix (IVM)	43
Figure 13. Homemade pendulum using a string and a nut	73
Figure 14. Pendulum held for dowsing	74
Figure 15. Directional guide for using a pendulum	75
Figure 16. Resonance analogy	78
Figure 17. Pendulums made of salt, flour, water + string	81
Figure 18. Pendulums made of acrylic (top) and wood (bottom)	83
Figure 19. How to find a pendulum's clockwise-rotation length (personal wavelength)	83
Figure 20. Holding the L-rod, with a counterclockwise rotation	87
Figure 21. Colors found by resonance in a sphere facing the sun and on circle drawn on paper, with compass directions indicated	95
Figure 22. The male and female polar elements seeking balance	107
Figure 23. Visualizing 3-6-9 in Torus / BG3 within Torus	186
Figure 24. The numbers 3-6-9 and BG3	188

Figure 25. 3-6-9 as vertical units ... 188

Figure 26. Yin Yang is part of the vertical cross-section of a torus ... 190

Figure 27. Yin Yang spiral in the torus (view from above) ... 190

Figure 28. Harmony from joining CW and CCW spiral ... 191

Figure 29. 3-6-9 and AUM ... 192

Figure 30. The Vortex Math structure ... 193

Figure 31. The Vortex Math Structure with connecting lines, producing 3-6-9 and BG3 ... 194

Figure 32. The Bagua structure ... 195

Figure 33. Reiki symbols ... 195

Figure 34. The Reiki power symbol (has BG3 and 3-6-9) ... 196

Figure 35. The L-90 structure and the 3-6-9 lines ... 197

Figure 36. Various torus structures (drawn clockwise) containing BG3 except in the center, which does have 3-6-9 ... 199

Introduction

Experiencing the deep realization that I, and every person, am the I AM changes everything.

What Led Me to Become the Seeker and Write This Book

For the past 18 years, I have been a seeker. I knew science and business, but at the age of 60, I discovered that I could feel and see "energies," something that was never discussed in the Western science I was taught. Here's how it came about:

I was at a yoga class, and the instructor had us warm up by doing a little qi gong exercise. We were told to build up and feel the qi energy at the center of our body between our palms, holding one hand at chest level and the other hand a little below the navel. To my surprise, I felt tingling in my hands, and then a feeling like a weight between my palms as I moved them up and down.

The next exercise was to send qi into the universe from our palms as a prayer. That evening at home, since I wanted to see if it was possible to view the qi that I had felt between the palms of my hand, I looked between my hands—and saw a fine, filament-like transparent "cloud" between them. As I went to bed that night, I held my palm up in the dark, and I could see the beam of energy, analogous to a beam of light, go out from my palm across the room to the wall. Being a scientist, since I did not know what I was seeing and experiencing, I went on a search to find the scientific basis of my observations.

Western Science Was Not Sufficient

I soon realized that Western science was not equipped to teach me anything about what I was observing. This inspired me to read everything relevant to the concepts of subtle energies so I could discover more about it. My studies included everything esoteric, ranging from concepts of creation, cosmology, metaphysics, quantum physics, healing, remote viewing, beliefs of yogis, different forms of meditation, mediumship and channeling, and many more topics.

I was hungry for experiences, since I believed that these would teach me more about the energies I was experiencing than if I just kept reading about them. As a result, I attended every type of healing modality event that I came across. Fairly soon, I joined the Foundation for Mind-Being Research (FMBR) so that I could learn from other folks who were also seeking.

Eventually, I would become the CEO and chairman of the Foundation for Mind-Being Research. But in the beginning, answers came slowly—answers as to the nature of reality. There were key teachers whom I met, and key books and courses, which taught me knowledge. Eventually, I realized that I was seeking enlightenment in order to feel the deepest sense of knowing. Such enlightenment came from various sources and teachers, and eventually from deep within me.

Realizing the "I AM"

I realized that I AM One with Source; that in essence, I am the "I AM," as is everyone.

Experiencing the deep realization that I, and every person, am the I AM changes everything. In this process comes an understanding of universal principles, such as: no judgment, compassion, forgiveness, and love. Realizing the "I AM" includes the realization that there is polarity in all of matter, and the need to find balance/harmony within the disharmony.

"I AM"—just two words, but such amazing words! (I will go into this topic in detail later in the book.) As an *ego* "I am," you may think of yourself as, for example: "I am a farmer," "I am a businessman," "I am a librarian," "I am a teacher," "I am a software engineer," "I am a doctor," etc. These are the ego titles or descriptions of yourself as you lead this life. (Chances are you have led many lives and worked at many professions.)

Introduction

But that is not the real you—your real essence. One main purpose of this book is to help you remember and understand the essence of who you really are. Your *essence* is truly the I AM.

My goal for the past few years, especially as the CEO and chairman of the Foundation for Mind-Being Research, has been to help people raise their level of consciousness so they also could understand who they truly are. When you experience an increase in consciousness, how you approach the world automatically changes. When there is a realization that we are all One, the problem of separateness is diminished in the world.

Encountering Joachim Wippich

And then I met Joachim Wippich. His work is central to this book.

I have now known him for years, having attended his lectures on dowsing at the San Jose Dowsers organization, where he teaches healing with the help of his special dowsing rods. He is also a frequent attendee at our FMBR lectures. My wife and I have been to his weekly Saturday noon gatherings at a coffee house in Cupertino, when people come to him for help in solving many health problems or just to listen to his wisdom.

While I have studied healing for many years, I discovered that Joachim truly embraced the nature of healing and the nature of who we are. He could see and measure the vibrational state of an individual and know if that person was at the I AM level, and where they were on their spiritual journey.

The purpose for Joachim's Saturday meetings is to help people to come to the Light. Joachim helps people see who they are and come into Harmony. When that occurs, *people automatically heal themselves.* Coming into Harmony is truly at the heart of healing and of understanding the Self.

In my mind, it is very important that Joachim's message be spread to the world. He has a unique way of delivering the message, and it is a gift that the world needs. Since Joachim's message and my message coincide, I decided to dedicate myself to writing his story, and also to put his message in the context of my understanding of the concepts I learned from my many years as a seeker for the truth of who we are. Joachim and I both came to the same conclusion.

Joachim's journey was by "divine download" of intuition, or direct knowing. As you reach the I AM state of being, you find that all information is there—you just have to remember it or ask for the knowing to present itself to you. This is Joachim's condition. He has led many previous lives, which have prepared him for this life and the teachings he now offers. In all likelihood, we have shared some lifetimes, since as soon as we met we experienced an instant bonding, based on our similar outlooks in life and knowingness.

My journey (which is detailed in Chapter 12) was guided by intuition and synchronicity, given to me a step at a time until the conclusion became obvious. My guides from the spirit side have guided me along a path leading to the current time, and to the writing of this book. I come to this conclusion because synchronicity has been guiding my steps throughout my life. Synchronicity is something that is guided, and not something that happens by chance. Intuition is what tells me to take *this* path versus *that* path, which leads me to where I am now.

Sharing Joachim's Wisdom and My Own Converging Views in This Book

This book describes Joachim's wisdom, the views that he and I share, and his concepts presented as affirmations. My journey taught me many concepts that I have experienced which have allowed me to reach this point in my life, and I hope that it will be of help to others along their journey.

In addition, I have been given information from divine intuition, which may help people understand the creation energies that surround us, and to help raise the level of consciousness. There is recognition/rediscovery of a new subtle energy quality that we can measure, and the associated science that may help the world. I have been calling this quality "3-6-9," since it resonates with 3-6-9 and structures associated with it. Nikola Tesla claimed that if we understood 3-6-9, it would help us understand the universe. In Chapter 13 you will learn that the 3-6-9 code is associated with creation. Its energy is within the key symbols of creation—the Sanskrit AUM, yin-yang, the torus structure, the power symbol used in Reiki healing, and the bagua from China. Use of 3-6-9 has a harmonizing quality. Joachim has used the quality of 3-6-9 in his affirmations with excellent results for healing, harmonization, and helping people to reach their I AM level.

What You Will Learn in This Book

The chapters in this book are structured to enable you to learn and understand fundamental concepts that will enable you to learn your true identity. You will learn:

- The fundamentals of achieving Harmony and why that is so very important. With that lesson, you will achieve a greater level of happiness.
- The nature of imbalance and why that causes illness on a personal level, breakup of relationships, political party dysfunctions, wars, and other problems. On a planetary basis, imbalances cause earthquakes, volcanoes, and hurricanes.
- How matter is formed and that all matter is formed in this manner.
- Why imbalances are inherent in the formation of matter and how you can bring it back to balance.
- How you interact with matter, but that the essence of you is not matter.

Joachim will teach you many "pearls of wisdom" and will give you affirmations to help you come into harmony and heal. His affirmations will enable you to reach the I AM level of vibration where you truly are at peace in the stillness of the connection to the center and to God. You will then know your connection to the Divine.

CHAPTER 1

Journey from Bending Spoons and Dowsing to Healing, and My Friend Joachim

Intuitively, what Joachim Wippich was really doing through dowsing was helping people come into harmony and raising the level of consciousness for the individual. That was what enabled people to heal.

In my early days as a member of the Foundation for Mind-Being Research (FMBR; *https://fmbr.org*), I attended my first spoon-bending party. This is a gathering where, by intention, you can cause metal to soften and turn it into a pretzel shape with no effort.

Edie Fischer, the host for the party, gave everyone a nut from a hardware store tied to a string. Holding the string vertically, with the nut weighting it down at the bottom, she said, "This is a pendulum. Say 'YES' and ask the pendulum to move in the 'yes' direction. Then say 'NO' and ask the pendulum to move in the 'no' direction. When you have established your 'YES' and 'NO' directions, pick up some spoons from this pile and ask your pendulum, 'Can I bend this spoon?' Then pick up some spoons from the 'Yes, I can bend this spoon' group and we will go through the instructions for bending the spoon."

I followed Edie's instructions, and the spoon that I picked up and told to bend softened, and I was able to bend it into a pretzel shape.

This exercise not only introduced me to the amazing ability of my consciousness/ intention to bend spoons, but it also introduced me to the fascinating field of *dowsing*. What we had just done with the pendulum was an illustration of dowsing. Intrigued, I asked members of FMBR where I could learn more about dowsing, and they told me about the San Jose Dowsers, which met monthly on the second Saturday at the Divine Science Community Center in San Jose, CA.

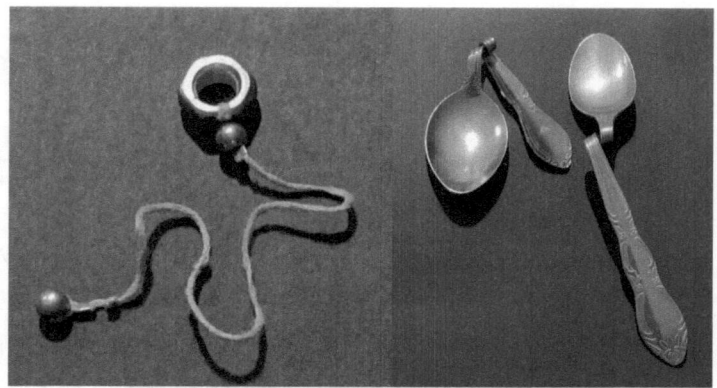

FIGURE 1. My first pendulum (a string and a nut), and some spoons turned into pretzels

Typically, people think about dowsers as people who look for places to dig wells for water, using Y-shaped sticks. Actually, *dowsing is a way to tap into the right brain, which has a lot of information.* A dowsing tool, such as a pendulum, allows one to access that information. Most people use dowsing to get a "yes" or "no" answer for specific questions, as we did when we picked the spoons that our pendulums indicated we could bend. There are other forms of working with pendulums for detecting energies. These are described in Chapter 3: You Are Not Just Your Body.

At the San Jose Dowsers meeting, I met a man named Pete Warburton, a dowser who could feel the energies and who used his fingers as the dowsing mechanism to support his abilities to do healing work. He would go to a coffee house in Cupertino on Saturdays at noon to help anyone in need of healing. I met with him and had many conversations to learn more about his techniques of using dowsing to help heal people. He had developed his own techniques to find where the traumas were located in individuals, and to release those traumas.

Meeting Joachim Wippich

Joachim Wippich was a dowser whom I met at the San Jose Dowsers organization. An emigrant from Germany, Joachim was a master at making machines—especially in the creation of optical parts—that solved problems no one else could solve. He eventually became an entrepreneur, creating a company to solve specialty problems in the Silicon Valley. After Joachim sold his company and retired, he picked up dowsing at the San Jose Dowsers club. With his machining skills, he soon developed his own special L-rod for dowsing. Joachim became interested in healing and in learning from Pete Warburton, since he specialized in using his dowsing skills for healing.

Intuitively, Joachim developed a different way of using dowsing for healing purposes. His technique actually had nothing to do with dowsing. Dowsing was just a tool to help focus the healing process and to tell about the true state of the person being healed. What he was really doing was helping people come into harmony and raising the level of consciousness for the individual. *That* was what enabled people to heal.

Pete would often confer with Joachim on difficult cases. Joachim would then work with the person, and he often obtained miraculous healings for a wide range of problems, such as physical pains, various diseases, stress-related problems, etc. His technique was to teach people to heal themselves. When Pete passed away a few years later, Joachim volunteered to be the new healer for the San Jose Dowsers.

It was during this time period that I met Joachim at the monthly dowsing meetings, where he would impart his wisdom and would help people heal. He and I have now known each other for many years and we have become good friends.

Joachim would also attend our monthly lectures at the Foundation for Mind-Being Research, where he and I would always get together. We enjoyed each other's company because we both understood the nature of who we are, "I AM," and we knew that this understanding was the basis for healing. Joachim also knew how to bring in Harmony, the basis for healing.

Over the years, I have watched Joachim heal hundreds of people. Joachim says he does not heal anyone; rather, he teaches people affirmations and how to finally understand his affirmations. The affirmations help people remember who they really are and to find harmony. With that understanding, true healing occurs. Once people understand Joachim's teachings, they can heal themselves at any time.

Spreading Joachim's Teachings

Joachim is a teacher. He is a teacher of the light, because he teaches that every person is of light, since they are the I AM. Once I understood the nature of his teachings, it became centrally important to me that his teachings would not be lost. The affirmations are the basis for healing and the reuniting of ourselves into the true I AM. Even though the message can be stated in a few sentences, there is a need for more information, since its simplicity may not be believable. That is because humanity, for the most part, has forgotten who we are.

Joachim is of German descent living in the US. English is his second language, and so it's much easier for me to try to tell his story than it would be for him. I have come to the same conclusions as Joachim, but from a completely different route (as I will describe in Chapter 12, "Journey of a Seeker"). I am hopeful that the convergence of our two routes will make Joachim's message more clear. That clarity will help move consciousness to another level, where healing, harmony, balance, happiness, and love become the standard way of being.

CHAPTER 2

Joachim's Central Message about Healing and Remembrance

Everyone becomes their own healer, since recognizing and understanding the simple points of Joachim's message results in healing.

Joachim's profound message about healing and remembering who we are is both extremely simple and yet difficult to comprehend. This is because we are not used to thinking in the manner he teaches. The meanings of these simple statements will be explained for you in this book.

The key messages are:
- We are our thoughts. We are the creators of our thoughts.
- Since matter has polarity, *we* have polarity. With polarity, imbalances can occur. Problems occur when there is loss of balance/harmony. Thus, healing often occurs when harmony and balance are re-established. Our cells may not know that they are in a state of disharmony, so when you invite them into harmony and let them know about the disharmony that is occurring, they will understand, and healing occurs.
- Recognizing and remembering who you are increases your vibrational state. You are not the ego "I am." You are the *eternal* "I AM." In fact, we *all* are the eternal "I AM."

Thus, everyone becomes their own healer, since recognition and understanding of these simple points results in healing. Joachim teaches affirmations on the above points. The words in his affirmations represent the thoughts (flow of thoughts), and often they do not follow good grammatical rules and may lack punctuation. But that doesn't matter: they result in the correct thought flow, and miracles will happen.

These affirmations may have to be repeated a number of times for the true meaning to sink into our conscious and subconscious minds.

One focus of this book is to achieve an understanding of the meanings of key words such as *I AM* and *Harmony*.

This book is called *The Seeker and the Teacher of Light*. I am "The Seeker," as I have been on a journey to reach a deeper level of knowing, and have come to the same truths as Joachim, but from a different direction. Thus, my story is included here along with Joachim's. Joachim is "The Teacher of Light," because he has remembered who he is.

CHAPTER 3

You Are Not Just Your Body

You are also spirit inhabiting your body.

There are some steps involved in learning what is meant by the term "I AM." The first step is to understand that you are NOT just your body. Yes, you *have* a body and it serves many functions that enable you to live on this physical plane. But you are more than simply your body.

And that is the purpose of this chapter: to share and discuss with you some of the major points to show that you are more than just the body — you are also spirit, inhabiting your body. Understanding that is the beginning of understanding I AM.

In our society, we are taught that the function of the brain, with the accompanying body, is you; that there is no "you" without the brain and body. Certainly, that is the predominant way science and medicine look at the definition of "you."

But that's only part of the equation. The brain is not necessarily identical to true consciousness. The brain may function more like an antenna, to receive messages in a certain way from the body. It has important functions, to be sure—but it's not all there is to you. Who you really are is much more than this.

Some of the Eastern cultures offer an alternative way to view who you really are. For example, when learning meditation in the Kriya Yoga school, as one inhales and exhales, one is taught to say "Hong Sau" (meaning, "I am Spirit"). The implication behind the words "Hong Sau" is that the body and brain are more like the clothes we wear in this lifetime. A deeper implication is that, as Spirit, we are immortal.

Kriya Yoga opens its practitioners up to subtle experiences that are available to everyone, but are not evident when focusing only on the world of the five senses, as we are taught to in the West. For example, you can learn to *hear* all the chakras: base chakra (motor or drum), sacral chakra (flute), lumbar chakra (harp or sitar), heart chakra (high-pitched bells), throat chakra (wind in the trees or waves of the ocean), spiritual eye chakra (symphony of the other chakras). In addition, with the spiritual eye (pineal), you see spiritual light and a five-pointed star as the third eye starts to awaken. Of course, they don't teach this until you have studied Kriya Yoga for some time, and have learned to meditate for at least four hours a day. But from the outset, they teach that you are not the body. With every breath you take, you are asked to think, "I am Spirit."

If we think we *are* our brain, we constrict our understanding of what we are truly capable of. Here are just a handful of examples of what people can do under the right conditions:

- People whose third eye has opened see more light than other people.
- People who are blind have been taught to read by means of subtle sensing, consciousness.
- Children have been taught how to see with their consciousness while being blindfolded; under this condition, they learned to read a book, play outdoors, and do other things that people would normally need their open, seeing eyes to do.
- Adults who had never done such things before were able to see things that were not in their immediate sight, accurately (remote viewing). (The film "Superhuman: The Invisible Made Visible" shows this and other experiences of extra-sensory perception.)

All this indicates that it's our *consciousness* that sees.

So when we are centered in who we really are—the I AM—we find that we are so much more than we thought we were. And this is the core of Joachim's healing approach, and the key message of this book.

I realize that the above paragraphs may be a lot to comprehend. Some of you will be tempted to stop reading at this point, throw up your arms, and say, "This is nonsense!" since this is so contradictory to everything you have been taught. But for those willing to read on, the understanding of who you are will free you to achieve deeper truths, which will free you from fear and enable you to know happiness, harmony, and greater health.

The sections below are intended to remind you that you are more than just your body.

What Quantum Physics Tells Us

In the world of quantum physics, it is common knowledge that the material world is not what it seems. Quantum physics says that the observer "collapses the wave," bringing about the reality of the observation. Although a quantum physicist would not use the term "creator," you are creating with your thoughts as you observe the world.

Scientists will tell you that everything you see is not really there in terms of "particles of matter." Any atom, molecule—or *you*—is 99.9999 percent not there. In essence, we are composed of waves and fields, much of which are electromagnetic. The feeling of solidness is likely nothing more than the repulsive forces of magnetism. In quantum physics, from the double-slit experiments (see below), we learn that it is the *observer* who determines whether what we perceive is a particle or a wave.

The Double-Slit Experiment

When electrons are fired through a slit with a particle detector on the other side, the electron behaves as a *particle*. When electrons are fired through two slits with a screen for wave detection, then *waves* are observed, as seen by the interference pattern formed. An interference pattern occurs when there is additive or subtractive interference of the wave going through the slits (see Figure 2).

Thus, at one level we are made of "particles," and at another level, we are "waves."

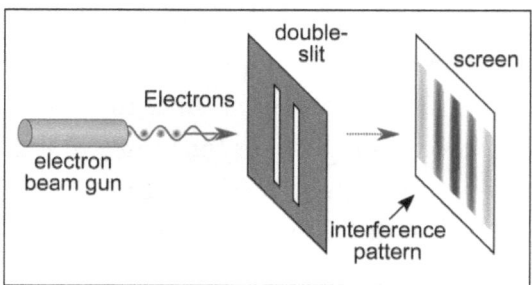

FIGURE 2. The double-slit experiment
Photons or particles of matter (like an electron) produce a wave pattern when two slits are used

The Implicate Order

Within the field of quantum physics, there are concepts such as the *invisible implicate realm*, which can form the physical world—the *explicate* realm. David Bohm, one of the primary quantum physics theorists, considered that what we take for reality are actually "surface phenomena, explicate forms that have temporarily unfolded out of an underlying implicate order" (i.e., the ground from which reality emerges). Stated another way, the *implicate realm* is where concepts, potentials, and archetypes are formed; and the *explicate realm* is where these concepts, potentials, and archetypes are materialized in the physical world. Other concepts in quantum physics include "collapsing the wave" to create in the physical world, i.e., the unseen wave becomes physical matter.

Quantum physics is real. Therefore it should make us question what exactly is "real" in terms of the material world.

The Brain: What It Is (and Isn't)

Another common belief in science and medicine is that we are the "brain." However, the brain is just the physical aspect of the mind.

Science writer Roger Lewin wrote a paper entitled "Is Your Brain Really Necessary?" in *Science*, describing the work of Dr. John Lorber, who studied the disease hydrocephalus. This is a condition where the water accumulates in the brain and crowds everything else out; that is, in the central part where the brain should be, it's largely water. In Lorber's time (he was born in 1915 and died in 1996), there was no simple way to drain the fluid in the brain. One would think the person would be completely incapacitated by this, but in Lorber's study, the people had normal thinking functions.

Lewin's paper on Lorber's work described nine persons who only had 5 percent of their brain tissue left; the rest of the brain was filled with fluids. Yet four of the nine had normal IQs, and two had IQs greater than 126! These studies have since been revisited, and although some of the brain tissue may be highly compressed, one has to question whether all of our brain functions/memories are actually stored in the brain. Our brain has the ability to pick up information, perhaps in the realm of the Akashic field (a term used to describe where all records are stored) or in the scalar energy waves around us. In some way, everything is stored out there, and it's our *access* to that and our ability to *gain that information* that works for us. We even have access to this kind of information even after the body has died. (*See* the section on "Death Is Just a Journey to Another Level of Vibration" later in this chapter.)

We can understand how minds work by considering how schools of fish swim or swarms of birds fly. Their brains don't tell them, "Turn left, turn right." (Think what kinds of traffic jams could result from that!) Instead of there being one leader guiding the group, the school or flock moves as one mind. This shows that there is more to how the "mind" communicates than simply the brain.

Some research scientists are beginning to approach this view. As science writer Peter Friederici wrote in *Audubon Magazine*, in the article, "How a Flock of Birds Can Flock Together":

> *Winging at speeds of up to 40 miles per hour, an entire flock of birds can make hairpin turns in an instant. How do they do it? A group of investigators is closer than ever to finding out.*
>
> The most impressive flockers are arguably those that form large, irregularly shaped masses, such as starlings, shorebirds, and blackbirds. They often fly at speeds of 40 miles or more per hour, and in a dense group the space between them may be only a bit more than their body length. Yet they can make astonishingly sharp

turns that appear, to the unaided eye, to be conducted entirely in unison. Imagine doing unrehearsed evasive maneuvers in concert with all the other fast-moving drivers around you on an expressway, and you get an idea of the difficulty involved.

University of Rhode Island biologist Frank Heppner, in the 1970s...suggested that they communicate through some sort of neurologically based "biological radio"....

Heppner speculates that there may be some fundamental math-based behavior going on—the kind of thing that physicists call an "emergent property," in which the whole is much greater than the sum of its parts.

We are all connected. On the level of consciousness, we are all of one mind. So when we're healing someone, it doesn't matter whether they are standing next to us or are 1,000 miles away. We're healing them through the one mind.

The Cleve Backster Experiments
We Communicate with All Life through Consciousness, and Distance Does Not Matter

In discussing how the "mind" works, and thus to give you a better idea of who we really are, it will help to talk about a few experiments. Let's start with the work of Cleve Backster.

Cleve Backster was a pioneer in the field of polygraphs (better known as "lie detectors"). In his later years, he had a commercial polygraph business. Earlier on, he had worked with the Central Intelligence Agency in the area of interrogation.

One evening, shortly after his secretary had purchased a plant for their office, Backster decided to connect the plant to his polygraph machine to see what would happen. He found that normal activities, such as tapping the leaf with a pen, did not produce any effect. However, when he thought about burning the plant with a match—even while he was standing 15 feet away—the plant gave a dramatic and strong signal from the polygraph machine.

Later, Backster learned that this same effect could be elicited from a stimulus many miles away—i.e., distance did not matter. He also learned that if he boiled live brine shrimp in the presence of the plant, the plant reacted. This proved to him that there is a level of consciousness in plants and other living systems, and that this consciousness can be tapped into by human consciousness.

This is not as strange as it might seem. We're connected to all the people, plants, animals, and everything in the world. Every atom in the universe is connected to everything else. We simply may not be aware of it.

The fact that Backster's experiments worked regardless of distance tells us that what's doing this kind of thing is the *mind*, the *consciousness*, not the physical body. The plant was responding to Backster's thought of burning it. So everything has an effect on everything else. And furthermore, the plant's reaction to the boiling of live brine shrimp indicates that it responded to the pain of *a whole other species*. (So a plant is not what we think, either.)

This oneness is the reality of the universe, and everything in it. But as humans, until both sides of our brain are in balance, we can't really experience that oneness. Right-brain consciousness is another form of consciousness in us. When we communicate only from the left brain, it doesn't recognize what the right brain does. In the above example, the left brain doesn't know "I'm communicating with a plant," but the right brain does. Until you get both sides of your brain into balance, it's hard to get that oneness to happen.

When the right brain and left brain are working together, you can coordinate the levels of the brain. An example: you may be in a crowded room with lots of noise, but if you can activate and harmonize the auditory aspect of the brain, suddenly you perceive the noise as just background noise, rather than cacophony. Similarly, your eyes can experience the EMFs (electromagnetic frequencies) of certain indoor lights as harmful to you; but if you learn to direct your eyes to come into harmony with the disharmony, they can come into balance and you are not negatively affected.

All this has a lot to do with coming into harmony, as you will see in Chapter 8.

Conscious Intention

The PEAR Lab Experiments on Intention and Random-Event Generators

We now know that the power of conscious intention can affect the material world. The Princeton Engineering Anomalies Research Laboratory (PEAR) was started by Dr. Robert Jahn to study the ability of consciousness to influence the physical world, specifically by experimenting with whether conscious intention would be able to affect sensitive electronic devices, including electronic random event generators (REGs). Working with Dr. Brenda Dunne, a developmental psychologist, and Dr. Roger Nelson, Dr. Jahn sought to explore the ability of test subjects to influence the random output distribution of these devices to conform to their intentions to produce higher numbers, lower numbers, or nominal baselines.

Their statistics proved, overwhelmingly, that conscious intent results in an effect on the random sequences. They found that merely by thinking, people could create non-random sequences among the numbers—whether they thought "increase," "decrease," or something else. They also proved, with their REGs, that events involving a group of people who have shared interests, such as sporting events and concerts, showed the greatest effect on readings from Random Event Generators.

This says that the mind has an effect on the material world.

Energies Surrounding a Person

Let's consider the aspect of energies surrounding and within a person.

Auras

Many clairvoyants see and read auras around another person. The *aura* is the energy surrounding the body. While not everyone can see auras, some people are sensitive to seeing them. They might, for example, see a glow in a darkened room.

Clairvoyants, however, see much more than this. They see the various bodies that all of us have, but which can be imperceptible to many. Many of those who see auras define the layers in the aura as being *etheric*, *emotional/astral*, *mental*, and *spiritual*. Clairvoyant Barbara Ann Brennan sees and defines 12 auric layers. Sometimes the auric layers are described as "bodies," so that one has an etheric body (which is closely associated with the physical body), then an astral or emotional body (which is much further away), followed by a mental body, then the spiritual or soul body. The etheric body, which is sometimes called the "energy body," vitalizes/energizes the physical body.

In regard to auras, there are colors surrounding the body, which books and articles describe. A dowsing teacher once advised me to look at a person against a white background, and when the person walked away I saw the complementary color. You see something that's actually there, but that you didn't see before. Clairvoyants see things that are there, which most people are not seeing.

I didn't used to see energies around people. However, now that I've started looking for them, I can see lines of energy above a person that I never realized were there, and I also *feel* energies. People do feel energies, even if they're not aware of it. In my experience, if I put my hands above someone else's and start moving my hands around, most of the people will feel the energy.

Kirlian Photography

Kirlian photography, a technique used to capture electrical coronal discharges on a photographic plate, was discovered by Semyon Kirlian in 1939. An object is placed on a photographic plate that's connected to a high-voltage source to produce an image on the photographic plate. This process reveals the energy patterns of plants and animals. This is a matter of setting out film and putting something on top of it, such as a leaf. The leaf has its own energies, and when the film is developed, you get an image of the leaf.

Interestingly, a plant being photographed in this way does not have to *be* intact and whole to *appear* intact and whole in the photograph. If you cut the leaf in half, put that on the film using Kirlian photographic techniques, let it sit awhile, then develop the film, often you will see the energetic image of the whole leaf. This "phantom leaf" phenomenon is well known; only part of it is visible, but its full energy is still there.

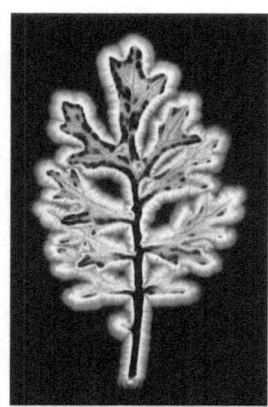

FIGURE 3. Kirlian photo of a dusty miller leaf

An immense advance over the Kirlian technique is Konstantin Korotkov's Gas Discharge Visualization (GDV) equipment. His experiments are documented in many hundreds of scientific papers. The equipment uses a weak electrical current applied to the fingertips for less than a millisecond. The fingertips form an "electron cloud" composed of light energy photons, which is measured.

Some people see just the etheric layer, which extends inches from the body. Some see the "lines of energy" between the hands. Many people feel the flow of energy in their bodies and between the hands. As for myself, I can see the etheric layer, feel the energy flow in my body, see and feel the rays emanating between my hands, and see the rays above everyone's heads.

In Tai Chi, practitioners play/dance with the ball of energy between the hands (the lines of energy between the hands that I mentioned earlier). I find that around 50 percent of people in the world can "feel" this energy. People will tend to *feel* energy—tingling, sensation, warmth, etc.—between the hands, even if they don't see it. If you tell people the energy is there, about 50 percent of them will begin to see it. People don't tend to know that such energies are there, so they don't see them. But if they look for it, they can start to see them.

Healers and Reiki practitioners often feel it. Healers, working with energy, are often able to help people to heal themselves. We are all more than just our physical bodies.

Chakras and Acupuncture Points

In addition to the above areas discussed, structurally the human body has a number of key energy centers. These are called *chakras*, or "wheels" (because they rotate). These energy vortices vary in size, with an average size of 3-4 inches. Chinese medicine has taught us about the meridians and acupuncture points. These are energy portals where the flow of energy can either flow or be blocked. These points and the meridian flows are well mapped. The use of acupuncture is now common in the Western world.

In addition, there are seven major chakras corresponding to the body, which run from the perineum to the crown of the head:

- The *root* chakra (your vital energy area)
- The *sacral* chakra
- The *solar plexus* chakra
- The *heart* chakra
- The *throat* chakra
- The *brow* chakra (pineal/third eye)
- The *crown* chakra

In *pranic energy healing*, 12 chakras are described, with slightly different terminology. Starting at the perineum, there is the basic chakra, and then in front of the body are the sex chakra, navel chakra, front spleen chakra, front heart chakra, throat chakra, ajna chakra, forehead chakra, and crown chakra on top of the head, with the Twelfth, or Golden Bud, chakra above the head. The back of the body has the back heart chakra, back solar plexus chakra, back spleen chakra, and the meng mein chakra.

Each chakra has its own characteristic and purpose, as well as a different tone and color. Eastern spirituality has known about chakras for ages.

Techniques such as Gas Discharge Visualization can evaluate the health of the main chakras. Dowsing can pick up the chakra energies and see how strong they are. They can be activated if they're not very active, and they can be centered. In Kriya Yoga training, one learns to listen to the "music" of the spinning chakras and to see the light within the third eye/pineal gland. The major chakras may be referred to as *energy centers* and are major acupuncture points, according to Master Choa Kok Sui. These chakras control and energize the vital organs and can control and affect psychological and spiritual conditions. There are also minor chakras. Master Choa's book, *The Chakras and their Functions*, states that there are 11 major chakras, some chakras on the front and some in the back of the body, with a twelfth chakra above the head, as mentioned above.

Innate Abilities

Most people have innate beyond-the-physical "abilities" in differing degrees. These never come to light because they have not tried using those abilities. Let's consider some of these innate abilities now:

Dowsing

Dowsing is typically viewed as being used to help you find something, such as water. But it's so much more than only that. It's really about how you use the ability of dowsing. You can use it for almost anything.

As long as you're in balance, it will give you information on what's in your right brain if you ask the dowsing tool (e.g., a pendulum) a question. You have to ask questions very exactly, however, because the right brain is very literal. For example, Joachim has found that if people say "Thank you so much," it lowers their vibrational level because "so much" is limiting (that is, there is a "more" that "so much" indicates just a portion of). So in dowsing, you have to ask the right question, so that the right brain understands specifically what you want. As long as you ask the question correctly and you're in balance, your right brain (by means of the dowsing tool) will give you the answer you want. It even will validate your answer by giving you a percentage, if you ask for it. You just get your pendulum going, and the pendulum will move and point to the correct-percentage answer.

If you're healing, you can dowse to find out what are the key problems, and even where they are located (e.g., in the physical body). Dowsing is an incredible tool for healing. Later, when we discuss I AM in Chapter 6, you will learn that the pendulum will rotate at the higher I AM vibrational level when you are at the I AM level of consciousness.

Dowsing organizations throughout the world teach this skill. Some uses of dowsing include: finding water, feeling the size of a person's energy field, and getting intuitive answers to questions.

The field of BioGeometry and the practice of radiesthesia use such tools to look at the energies that surround us. BioGeometry is the science of using shape (as well as colors, motion, orientation, and sound) to balance/harmonize biological energy systems and their interactions with the environment. Radiesthesia is the science of tuning into the vibrational energy of the human body or other objects, whether animate or inanimate, to establish resonance with their energy fields, using pendulums or other instruments.

Radiesthesia differs from mental dowsing. In mental dowsing, you are consciously asking a question so that the right brain can provide you with an answer. In radiesthisia, you are not asking a question. Instead, you are using the pendulum as a tool to detect resonance at the level of awareness. To determine your personal wavelength, you drop the pendulum from its base to the length at which it rotates clockwise by itself (since it is then in resonance with you). You have not asked a question. If, for example, you are connecting the rotation of yourself (personal wavelength) to a supplement, then if the rotation goes clockwise by itself, the supplement is in resonance with you and is thus good for you. Again, you have not asked a question, you have merely looked at the resonance between yourself and the supplement.

In radiesthesia, you can use a neutral pendulum (*see* Chapter 8: "Dowsing, Harmony, and the Vibrational Level") to determine the resonance of practically anything. For example, if you have an electron micrograph of a virus, you can determine the string length of the pendulum that is in resonance with the virus (the string length that causes the pendulum to rotate clockwise). If you have a picture of a person who has that virus in their body and you put that picture with the picture of the virus, the pendulum will rotate clockwise (i.e., the person is in resonance with the virus). If the person does not have the virus, the rotation will not happen. The picture of the person is a "witness" of the person; you are in resonance with the person through the picture.

In BioGeometry, it was determined that subtle energies of the center are harmonizing. Those same energies are found in sacred spots throughout the world. Radiesthesia was able to determine the resonant qualities that were present in those spots and in the center. Tools were developed that had the resonant qualities of the center and sacred spots, and were able to bring about harmonization and, thus, immense benefit for people using such tools.

Remote Viewing

This is the ability to know where someone or something is. You can ask, "I want to know what's at this coordinate," or for a person at a distal location, "I want to know what that person is seeing or feeling." There are remote-viewing techniques to enhance this ability. Later on, when you compare what you received in asking this question with what the person was *actually* seeing and feeling, the degree of similarity is remarkable. Remote viewing is an ability that a lot of people can have, if properly trained.

The American physicist Russell Targ worked at the Stanford Research Institute, doing remote viewing studies sponsored by intelligence agencies. He made a documentary called "Third Eye Spies," which I strongly suggest you watch. The film describes the many experiments carried out by Targ and his associates at the Stanford Research Institute. Remote viewing has been extensively used by both US and Russian intelligence agencies with a high degree of accuracy. When President Carter was wondering whether Russians could locate hidden missiles being moved around on trucks, remote viewing showed that the locations of those missiles could be found, wherever they happened to be. This resulted in the end of the program to hide missiles on trucks.

Healing

In this chapter, we are discussing alternative healing for restoring health when there is an imbalance, disease, or damage. This is distinct from the standard allopathic medicine practiced in the Western world.

There may be some commonalities among the different alternative healing modalities. For example:

- Distance does not matter (non-locality): That healing can take place even over distances indicates our connectedness.
- Involvement with subtle energy: Examples of subtle-energy modalities include qi, touch, torsion waves, subtle energy connection, and Reiki.
- Many aspects can be involved in enabling the modalities to work: For example, color, angles, sound, light, shapes, torsion energies, BioGeometry.
- Being a healer may be a universal human ability.
- Some techniques are informational, involving communication from the subconscious to the conscious mind: Examples include Emotional Freedom Technique (EFT) and BodyTalk.
- Combinations of modalities can be used: For example, Radionics, Radiesthesia.

Here is just a partial list of healing modalities:

- Reiki
- Sound
- Light
- Color (seeing colors and projecting them); BioGeometry; Quantum Wave
- Quantum (Matrix Energetics): Richard Bartlett
- Qi/Chi
- Spiritual: Jane Katra
- The Connection: Eric Pearl
- Quantum Touch: Richard Gordon
- Torsion/Scalar Waves
- Bengston Approach
- BioGeometry Approach: Harmonization
- Crystals
- Programming metals and minerals with subtle energy: Yury Kronn (Vital Energy Technology)
- BodyTalk
- Radiesthesia
- Radionics
- EFT (Emotional Freedom Technique)
- Hands of Light: Barbara Brennan

- Acupuncture: clearing blocks
- Harmony and Dowsing: Joachim Wippich
- Dalian Method: Mada Dalian
- BioGenesis
- Shamanism
- Pranic Healing

It is not the purpose of this book to describe all healing techniques, since each method has a significant story. However, books *have* been written about all these techniques. I will mention a few stories to show that the human ability of healing is inherent in all of us.

- *Body Talk:* This modality uses the healing technique of learning from the body what the problem might be. In this method, the healer learns how to "hear" the nature of the problem by "feeling" the message from the body. Healing is then just a matter of the conscious mind's recognition of the problem.
- *Eric Pearl's "Reconnective Healing":* Pearl simply uses his hands to establish an energetic connection to the people being healed. With this kind of healing, you're not using physical objects but rather your connective ability to the person. The healing may be happening through *subtle energies*.
- *Qi:* Qi Gong masters and other healers use the subtle energy of qi. It works, and it defies the logic of Western medicine.
- *Bengston Technique:* Bill Bengston's story is interesting. A scientist at a university, he had a friend who was a healer who healed with his hands. The friend was planning to do a healing experiment with cancer and mice at his university, but at the last minute he left. This left Bill to do the experiment, based only on what he had seen his friend do, using his hands. And so he did. He watched the tumors get dark and worse—and then suddenly they fell away, and none of the mice died. From this, Bengston developed a technique to condition a certain healing state of mind, which he used to heal mice with cancer. He went on to teach graduate students how to do this. His book, *The Energy Cure: Unraveling the Mystery of Hands-On Healing*, describes

this technique. One key message in the book is that everyone has the ability to heal, and that the ability can be taught.

Clearly, there is more to who we are and our abilities than is commonly assumed. Those who know how to use those innate abilities are able to perform amazing feats: for example, yogi masters and Buddhist monks are able to suspend their breathing for extended periods of time. All this reminds us (or clues us in for the first time) that we are more than our bodies.

Death Is Just a Journey to Another Level of Vibration

The fear that limits most people and clouds their outlook in life is the fear of death. People tend to count their lives in terms of days and years. If they do not believe in an afterlife, they may take the stance of grabbing whatever they can in life and not caring about others. Such a stance may be taken not only by individuals, but also by governments and nations.

However, if one looks deeper, the fear of death is not based on anything true. There *is* no true "death"; we just move on to other planes of existence. The evidence is here for those willing to look. Here is just some of the evidence:

Near-Death Experience (NDE)

Many people have gone through a NDE. You can usually find someone in almost any group who has had this experience. In the worldwide branches of the International Association for Near-Death Studies (IANDS), people freely describe their near-death experiences.

Their stories have a lot of commonalities. Typically, their deaths involve:

- An out-of-body experience (see below)
- Movement through a tunnel to the light on the other side
- Life reviews (sometimes)
- Experiencing deep love
- The desire to not return to physical life but instead to remain on the other side. If the deceased person is instructed to return to

life, they often come back dramatically changed. They no longer fear death, they understand immortality, and they understand the depth of love present on the other side.

Out-of-Body Experience (OBE)

During an OBE, the person can travel in the current physical plane or to the different planes of the spirit world. They can even meet loved ones who have passed away.

An out-of-body experience can take place when you are sleeping, or when there's a trauma. Typically, you are in a hypnogogic state (between being awake and asleep), in which the body goes into paralysis. You may hear noise, and things may seem to be rumbling and shaking—and suddenly you are outside your body, looking down at it.

If you get scared, you come right back into the body. But if you allow yourself to go out, you can travel into another room, or into the afterlife. If you're very advanced, you'll be able to communicate and be with people in other realms and dimensions. You also can communicate with your higher Self in a better, more comprehending way.

It can happen naturally. Sometimes, when you're dreaming about flying, you may actually be having an OBE.

OBEs are more common than you might expect. In almost any group of people, typically you will find someone who has had an OBE but is reluctant to talk about it, or may even be afraid of the experience since they do not understand it.

One thing to be learned from OBEs is that when you're dead, you're still alive; you're just in another realm. It's just that the parameters have changed.

For those who are interested in learning more about OBEs, there are several places that teach the techniques of achieving the OBE experience, such as the International Academy of Consciousness (IAC) and the Monroe Institute. Robert Monroe was the pioneer of understanding OBEs, using a method of "hemi-sync"—a process used to create audio patterns containing binaural beats—to make it happen. His more recent book, *A Far Journey*, makes for fascinating reading.

Mediums and Channeling

Mediums are people who bring in the voices and thoughts of people who have passed over to the other side. Some mediums transmit the essence of what people on the other side want to tell the inquiring person on this side. Others let the person on the other side come directly into them, so that the being can speak through them using his or her own lingo, skills, and talents.

There are some wonderfully talented mediums who are able to connect to beings on the other side. The information they bring back is often amazing. On the website *www.ChallengerCC.org*, you can hear the story of the *Challenger* shuttle astronauts who perished in 1986. The main message they wanted to tell the world and their loved ones is that "there is no death."

The astronauts who died in the *Columbia* shuttle also were recently channeled. Their story, in their own words as brought through by two wonderful mediums, also can be heard on the *ChallengerCC.org* website. You can also link to that website through the *FMBR.org* website. FMBR (Foundation for Mind-Being Research) also has a project with Mark Ireland, author of *Messages from the Other Side*, to bring together a list of qualified talented mediums able to communicate with the deceased on the other side.

Electronic Voice Phenomenon (EVP) and Instrumental Trans-Communication (ITC)

Dan Drasin has created a wonderful documentary, "Calling Earth," about afterlife communication via modern electronic technology. Spirits are able to manipulate electronic devices (radios, TV, cameras, recorders, phones, etc.) to send messages. There are groups that research this and listen to it. See: *https://vimeo.com/101171248*

Hypnosis and Regression

Past life regression is a method that uses hypnosis to recover memories of past lives or incarnations. Dr. Raymond Moody has done extensive research on near death experiences, the nature of the afterlife, and past life regressions. His book *Life after Life* is wonderful recommended reading. Dr. Michael Newton, a hypnotherapist, has written an excellent book, *Journey of Souls*, about the nature of spirit life between reincarnations.

In Conclusion

All the information provided in this chapter gives evidence that we are more than just a body, that physical reality is not always what it seems, and that there is life after death. In short, we are eternal spirit.

Summary of Key Points in This Chapter

All the information provided in this chapter gives evidence that we are more than just a body, that physical reality is not always what it seems, and that there is life after death. In short, we are eternal spirit.

- In this chapter, we learned that our essence is not the body and brain. It is the eternal I AM.
- In quantum physics, we learned that matter is not what it seems—it can be a particle or a wave, depending on the observer. We are a creator of what we see.
- Our consciousness does not reside in the brain. People with hydrocephalus may have more water than brain tissue, yet may have normal intelligence.
- Conscious intent influences outcomes, as seen in the PEAR lab experiments.
- We are more than our bodies, as seen by our auras and chakras. Kirlian photography and Gas Discharge Visualization experiments show the energy pattern surrounding matter—both living and non-living—when given an electric charge. We have the ability to go beyond the physical, as seen in our ability to dowse, to remote-view distant locations, and to heal, even at a distance.
- The experiments with Cleve Backster demonstrate our ability to communicate with plants, even at a distance.

- We are eternal, as evidenced by the near-death experience (NDE), out-of-body experience (OBE), channeling, and hypnotic regression of previous lives.

CHAPTER 4

As Above, So Below — The Formation of Matter

All matter is created in the same manner.

There is a phrase we sometimes hear: "As above, so below." This means: "What happens on one level of reality also happens on every other level; the microcosm and macrocosm behave alike."

This statement becomes very important as we study the mechanism of the creation of matter. Having a grasp of the concept of how matter is formed provides vital clues as to the nature of our bodies, the planet, and every part of the physical universe. This understanding will give us further insight into who we truly are, as well as what I AM means.

The purpose of this chapter is to give insights into the nature of how matter is created.

Within all matter, we learn there are attractive and repulsive forces. This can be thought of as *gravitational* and *magnetic* forces. In the newer theories of matter formation, which we will be discussing, gravitational forces may be vortex motion *into* a center, and magnetic forces may be vortex motion *out of* a center.

In this chapter, I will share the theories of key individuals who teach us that *all matter is created in the same manner*.

The Vortex Motion of Light, and Creation

The vortex motion of light (can be speculated to be the "quantum fluid" or "aether") into and out of the center is a fundamental aspect of creation. Matter is created by the compression of light in a centripetal motion inward (a vortex), and the dissipation of matter radiates outwards in a centrifugal motion. This is analogous to winding up a spring in a clock. The spring is unwound at the beginning (i.e., it is less dense); as it winds, it becomes more compact; and when fully wound, it is very compact (i.e., very dense). Substitute the word "light" or "quantum fluid" for the spring, and you get the idea. When light is dense, it is matter.

This motion is the basis of a spherical *toroidal* structure. A *torus*, which has the appearance of a donut, is the shape of spiraling light (energy) compressing into a center. (In geometry, *torus* is defined as a surface or solid formed by rotating a closed curve—especially a circle—around a line that lies in the same plane but does not intersect it.) These are rotations that compress down to a denser portion in the center, which is the process of creating the densities that are matter. All light/quantum fluid is compressed and passes through the center. This center is the point of maximum spiraling, greatest density, maximum vibration, and the point of stillness. Imagine a glass of water vibrating — it sloshes around. But at some point, the vibration is sufficiently high that the water appears not to be moving at all. (We will go into the torus in more detail later on in this chapter.)

FIGURE 4. Model of a torus

Another interesting point is that everything that is spiraling passes through the center. Anything that goes into a torus will go through the center and out again. The center sees everything, since everything that's on the surface goes through the center. Because everything is created from the center, everything is in the center, so everything comes to a point. Everything that goes out recycles back into the point. So the point has the potential of everything: all knowledge, all potentialities.

Figure 4 (previous page) is a model of a torus I made from a clothes-dryer duct. The cover is of cloth that has been colored with seven colors. As you rotate the torus inward toward the center, all the colors will pass through the center.

What Brings About Harmony and Disharmony

Now, to bring quantum science and the spiritual world together (as Walter Russell's ideas, below, reveal), the underlying centering/balancing force behind the toroidal vortex motion of matter is God, or the consciousness of God.

"God" is the centering of all this energy. Like the two ends of a seesaw, God is centering, keeping things balanced. Therefore, everything is of God (of this torus structure). Matter is the spiraling compression of the vortex, balanced by God. We have the consciousness we do because we are the thought-creation of God, and our consciousness is of God. We are part of that cosmic ocean. God is the omniscient, omnipotent ocean that is all. We think we're separate, but we are a wave of that ocean that is God.

There is harmony or balance when matter—which includes our bodies—is aligned with the center. The further we deviate from the center, the greater the disharmony. Our problems occur when we believe that we are separate from our Creator and behave in ways that deviate from harmony and balance.

It's so important for humans to understand that there is no separation between ourselves and God. People have lost this understanding because they have identified themselves as individual egos, which they believe are separate. They do not realize they are a wave of the ocean that is fully connected. As we awaken and learn that we are a part of God, we open to our true identity and potential and to Harmony and Love.

A corollary to this is that for anything to exist, there must be some level of consciousness. For matter to form, God is there, balancing the spiraling vortices of light. Thus, all matter has some level of consciousness (awareness) since every manifestation of matter is part of the conscious ocean that is God. All rocks, atoms, plants, animals are of God, with differing levels of awareness. Humans are more aware, and are starting to realize that they are not separate but a part of God. Humanity will also then realize that everyone and everything is connected; we are all part of the One.

We are formed in balance, but many forces can cause unbalance. For humans, it can be thoughts/perceptions, toxins, diseases, conflicts with others, etc. We must learn the principles of harmony to bring back balance. The air, water, and earth can also go out of balance, and forces will occur to bring back balance. (This will be gone into more deeply in the chapter on Harmony and Balance, and the chapter on the healing work of Joachim Wippich.)

However, it's only our physical bodies that are of matter. Our *essence*, our consciousness, is not of matter. We are spirit. Even when we die, although our original physical body is no longer there, our essence or consciousness is here. That's why when people have a Near-Death Experience, they experience themselves as being here.

Walter Russell's View of Creation

It can help us understand all this by seeing how Walter Russell looked at the nature of creation. In Russell's work, two aspects of light (blue and red) spiral to form matter. In addition, there is the aspect of the cycle of *matter disintegration* (radiation), which is then again followed by the cycle of creation.

Walter Russell (1871-1963) was a polymath — excelling as a painter, sculptor, author, philosopher, musician, champion figure skater, and scientist. His paintings and sculptures are in the main galleries in Washington, D.C. An excellent biography of Russell is Glenn Clark's book, *The Man Who Tapped the Secrets of the Universe*. Some of Russell's own books include: *The Secret of Light*; *The Message of the Divine Iliad*; *A New Concept of the Universe*; and *The Universal One*; *In the Wave Lies the Secret of Creation*.

His great flash of inspiration came from a pilgrimage in the woods, of which he says:

> I will put it very simply. In May of 1921, God took me up into a high mountain of inspiration and intense ecstasy. A brilliant flash-like lightning severed my bodily sensation from my consciousness and I found myself freed from my body and wholly in the Mind universe of Light, which is God.

For Walter, the message from God was:

> And then God said to me, "Behold thou the unity of all things in Light of Me, and the seeming separateness of all things in the two lights of my divided thinking. See thou that I, the Undivided, Unchanging One, am within all divided things, centering them, and I am without all changing things, controlling them."
>
> And the secrets of the universe were unfolded to me in their great simplicity as the doors to the Light opened fully to my consciousness. In less time than it takes to put it into words, I knew all there was to know of the CAUSE of all effect, for there was very little to know. In that hour it was as though the infinity of complexity within the moving kaleidoscope was suddenly taken apart and it was shown to me that the entirety of its illusion was but three mirrors and a few bits of broken glass.
>
> Likewise, the universal kaleidoscope was but moving mirror waves of dual light extending from their equilibrium in God from whom all creating things spring in octave electric waves just as ocean's waves spring from the calm sea.
>
> Thus knowing the static Light of God, and the two dynamic lights of His thinking, and the electric processes by means of which His thinking is recorded in "matter," I at once had the key to all the sciences, mathematics, chemistry, astronomy and mechanics, likewise all the underlying principles of creation; of life and the healing principle; of continuity in a universe in which there is no death; of energy which is not what man thinks it to be; and of matter which is not substance as man supposes it to be; and of the forces which act upon it which man has learned how to use somewhat but knows not the why of that which he uses.

For very many days and nights I was made to write down all these things which I knew in *The Divine Iliad*, which is my record of my teachings while in the Light. And in that one volume of many thousands of words there was never an erasure nor correction; and the language of that divine message was not mine. I could never have written such rhythmic essence of knowledge, nor have created its exalted style.

By this rarest of all experiences ever to happen to any man, it was made known to me just what Jesus meant when He spoke of "the Light of the world." He meant just that, yet it has been misinterpreted as metaphor, or symbol.

No greater proof than my experience is needed to prove to the doubting world that all knowledge exists in the Mind universe of Light — which is God — that all Mind is One Mind, that men do not have separate minds, and that all knowledge can be obtained from the Universal Source of All-Knowledge by becoming One with that Source.

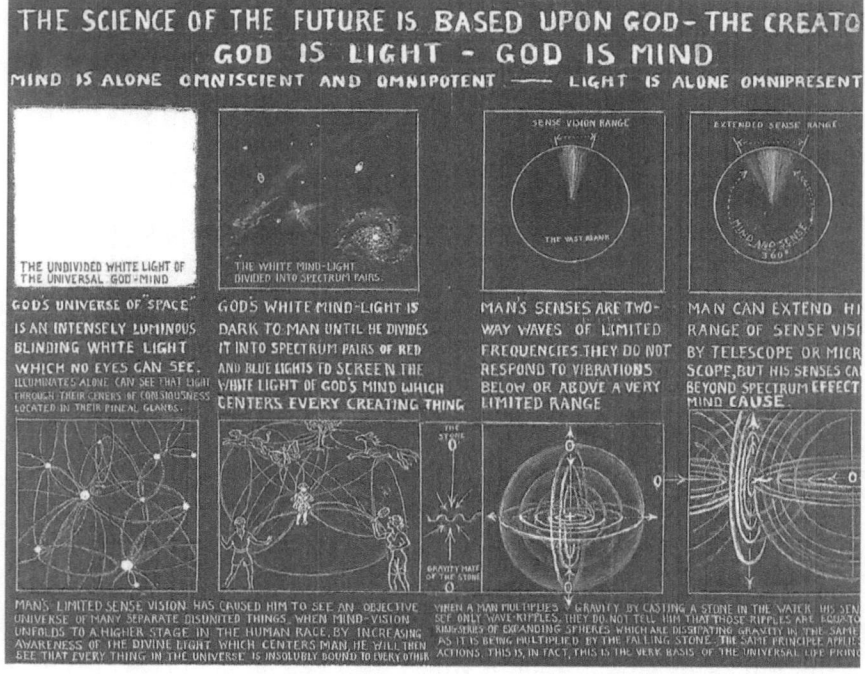

FIGURE 5. Walter Russell's view of creation

The set of pictures, above, created by Russell, are the best to explain the Oneness of God and all Mind.

In case you can't fully read or decipher what's in this illustration, this is what Russell says at the outset:

> The Science of the Future Is Based upon God—The Creator. God Is Light —God Is Mind. Mind is alone omniscient and omnipotent—Light is alone omnipresent.

And in terms of the images, he says (what's in quotes; my explanations follow the close quotes, or stand alone):

Top row (left to right):

- *Left-most:*

    "The Undivided White Light of the Universal God-Mind. God's universe of 'space' is an intensely luminous blinding white light which no eyes can see. Illuminates alone can see that light through the centers of consciousness located in their pineal gland."

- *Second from left:*

    "The White Mind-Light Divided into Spectrum Pairs. God's white mind-light is dark to man until he divides it into spectrum pairs of red and blue lights to screen the white light of God's mind which centers every creating thing."

    This shows that we can see only a small spectrum of the light. What God did was to take just a small fraction of the light (the spectrum between red and blue). Therefore, everything appears dark except the narrow spectrum that we can see. But we're really part of everything.

- *Third from left*:

    "Sense Vision Range / The Vast Blank. Man's senses are two-way waves of limited frequencies. They do not respond to vibrations below or above a very limited range."

    This shows the narrow spectrum that we *can* see—the spectrum between blue and red. Similarly, we can only "hear" within a limited range.

- *Fourth from left*:

  "Extended Sense Range / Mind and Sense." Man can extend his range of sense vision by telescope or microscope, but his sense cannot go beyond spectrum EFFECT into mind CAUSE."

  Again, this shows the narrow spectrum that we *can* see — the spectrum between blue and red, which is the range shown between "sense vision range" in the figure.

Bottom row (left to right):

- *First and second from left*:

  These pictures show that we can see only the separateness of things, due to our limited vision. But in fact, they are insolubly bound to each other, as shown by the connecting lines between stars or between individuals and animals. Whatever we look at (e.g., stars) look separate, like dots; but it's all part of the white light. Everything is connected. We're all part of that white light, we're all One; we just think we're separate things that are out there.

- *Third and fourth from left*:

  The last two images show the principle of waves. If you throw a stone into water, you see only the surface ripples; you miss the three-dimensional interactions of the waves, a structure with all the complex ways in which things interact. That's how *we're* made. We are also waves and fields.

As Russell concludes:

Man's limited sense vision has caused him to see an objective universe of many separate disunited things. When mind-vision unfolds to a higher stage in the human race, by increasing awareness of the Divine Light which centers man, he will then see that everything in the universe is insolubly bound to every other thing. Science will then know that matter is but many focal points of one body.

When a man multiplies gravity by casting a stone in the water, his senses see only wave-ripples. They do not tell him that those ripples are equatorial ring series of expanding spheres which are dissipating gravity in the same ratio as it is being multiplied by the falling stone. The same principle applies to all actions. This is, in fact, this is the very basis of the Universal Life Principle.

And he adds, wryly: "Science has built a strange universe from sense evidence, and has been mightily deceived."

Centrifugal and Centripetal Spiral Compression

In his various books, Russell explains that *the nature of creation is based on clockwise centripetal spiral compression of two equally opposed large volumes of light waves to form matter.* The breakdown of matter is the counterclockwise centrifugal spiral radiation for unwinding matter. Matter creation and its disintegration is an unending cycle of waves.

The next images show these principles. The first image shows the clockwise centripetal gravitational vortex inward to the center of the two lights, red and blue, which is the basis of the creation of matter. Their disintegration occurs by counterclockwise centrifugal radiation (rotation not shown in this diagram).

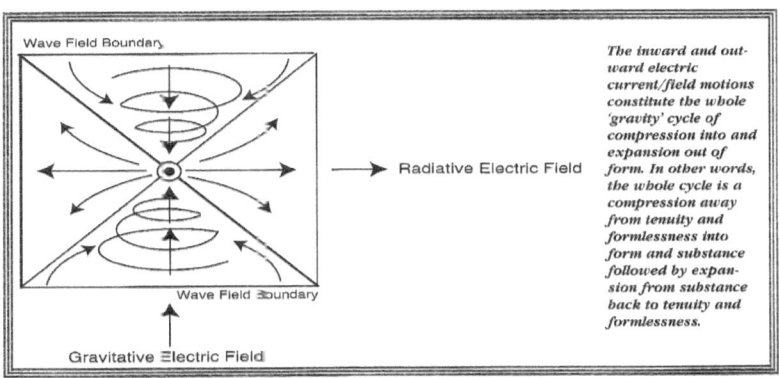

FIGURE 6. The basis of the creation of matter
*Clockwise centripetal gravitational vortex inward
to the center of the two lights, red and blue*

Russell's caption reads:

The inward and outward electric current/field motions constitute the whole "gravity" cycle of compression into and expansion out of form. In other words, the whole cycle is a compression away from tenuity and formlessness into form and substance, followed by expansion from substance back to tenuity and formlessness.

What does this mean? You see the vortex motion coming into the center from both sides (the red light and the blue light). This is the centripetal motion. As matter forms, things become more dense. Since everything is a cycle, matter will dissipate; this is radiation, or centrifugal motion outwards.

- Gravitational forces push things together.
- Then it dissipates out.
- Then it will recycle: physical matter will come back in to form the vortex again.

It's a cycle, a wave of creation, dissipation / creation, dissipation / and so on. Nothing ever disappears. Matter radiates away (back to the ocean of white light), and then recycles back again as matter.

But our essence is not of that light, so *we* don't disappear; we're part of God. We are part of the ocean that has individuated but is not separate. Everything is eternal.

The same principle, shown with a picture of the cones of the vortex, appears at right.

Russell's captions read:

All vortices turn from west to east and their apices point to north.

Mass is accumulated around a vortex. A vortex is formed by the contraction of the axes of two opposing cones of energy. The greater the contraction, the greater the acceleration of motion within the vortex.

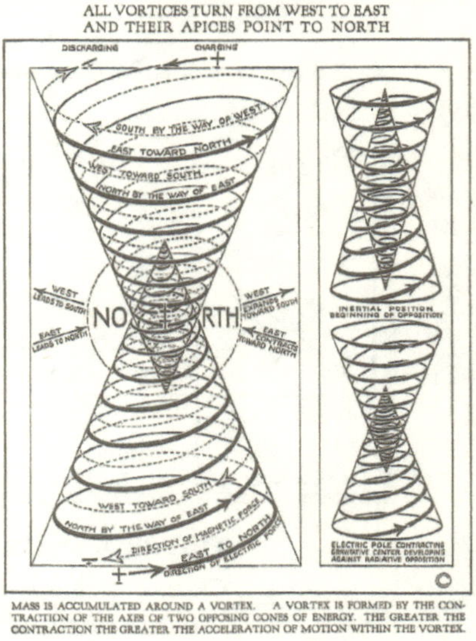

FIGURE 7. The basis of the creation of matter: the cones of the vortex

Another diagram showing this same principle (with slightly different terminology to describe the concept of formation [integration] and disintegration) is shown below. In Russell's terminology, "N" is North, the direction to the center where mass is formed, and "S" is South, the direction of radiation for disintegration of matter.

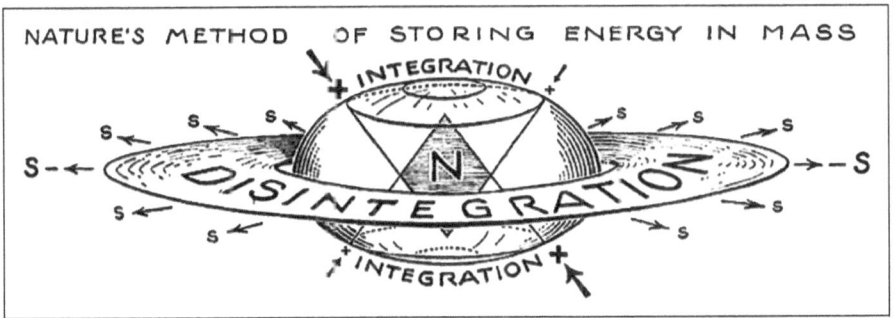

FIGURE 8. The basis of the creation of matter: Nature's method of storing energy in mass

These diagrams are all speaking to the same thing.

Light is spiraling in to form the denseness of matter. That's integration—gravity compressing matter. Compressed light spiraling out is the disintegration of matter.

Summary of Walter Russell's Matter Creation through Light

In his various books, Walter Russell explains that *the nature of creation is based on clockwise centripetal spiral compression of two equally opposed large volumes of light waves to form matter*. On the other hand, *the breakdown of matter is the counterclockwise centrifugal spiral radiation for unwinding matter*. Matter creation and its disintegration is an unending cycle of waves.

The essence of Russell's finding is that creation of matter is based on causing light to be divided into polar parts (his terminology is "male and female colors of red and blue"), and compressing them by centripetal vortex pressures (clockwise). Voiding of matter then occurs by centrifugal vortex expansion/unwinding (counterclockwise). This is an eternal cycle of creation and voiding (disintegration), recycling what is voided to create matter again.

A Clairvoyant Understanding of the Atom

Russell's description has similarities to how the nature of an atom was described by clairvoyants Charles Leadbeater and Annie Besant, members of the Theosophical Society. They investigated the nature of atoms through clairvoyance between 1895 and 1933. Their description of the atom appears in their book, *Occult Chemistry: Investigations by Clairvoyant Magnification into the Structure of the Atoms of the Periodic Table and Some Compounds*. In this book, they described what they called the "Anu" (also called the UPA, for the "Ultimate Physical Atom"): the basic building block of matter—the spiral motion of the aether, as pictured below. (The *aether* is a dense, fluid-like medium, now often called the *quantum fluid*.) The Anu structure is definitely reminiscent of the vortex structure described by Walter Russell. It is interesting to note that there is a male and female spiraling torus. This would be equivalent to Walter Russell's two opposing torus structures of male red light and female blue light. It is also equivalent to the double torus described by Nassim Haramein in the next section.

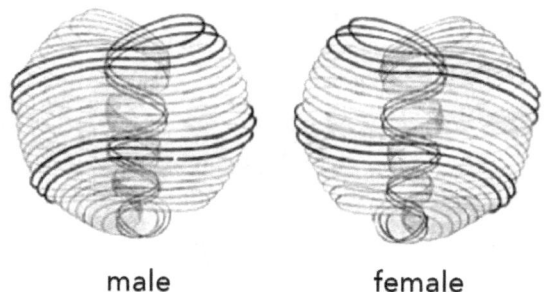

male   female

FIGURE 9. The "Anu"—the basic building block of matter—the spiral motion of the aether

The Torus Structure

The spiraling vortex motion results in the formation of a *torus structure*.

The torus structure is fundamental to the basis of creation. As Arthur Young wrote in his book, *The Reflexive Universe*, "The torus is a doughnut-shaped whirlpool vortex that is the only manner by which self-sustained motion can exist in a given medium." This means that the torus is the only form in all of nature where the flow of energy through it is continuously sustained. This allows it to keep its shape at any scale.

The torus is the form that sustains creation from the micro to the macro — from subatomic particles through galactic clusters, and beyond. It is the shape of the electro-magnetic field of an atom, a seed, a human, a planet, a solar system, a galaxy and—it's now being reported—the Universe itself.

Foster Gamble, a writer and film producer who glimpsed what he perceived to be the Universe's fundamental energy pattern while he was still in his teens, offers wonderful graphics and descriptions of the torus on his website: *www.thrivemovement.com*. The graphics show the torus structure as being basic in: *astronomy* (from solar systems, to galaxies, to the universe); *chemistry* (toroidal vortices combining to form atoms and molecules); *biology* (molecules forming cells, which comprise life); and in *humans* (our central core surrounded by electromagnetic fields, as well as our finer toroidal subtle bodies — etheric, astral, mental, and spiritual levels).

Matter is a function of the spiraling motion in the aether (also called the "zero point energy field" and, more recently, the "quantum fluid"). The primary pattern of motion is the torus vortex, and which part of it we are looking at determines the force. In other words, *electricity, magnetism, gravity, and the strong and weak nuclear forces all are different parts of the torus*. Electricity could be considered the rotation around the center. Magnetism could be the *push out* at one end of the torus, and gravity could be the *pull into* the torus.

The work of Nassim Haramein, the founder of the Resonance Science Foundation, postulates that black holes (formed by an intense gravitational field) are at the center of every torus system, from atoms to galactic clusters; they are just different sizes.

We have black holes in us, in our atoms. Atoms, hydrogen, oxygen, and so on are all centered in black holes. These black holes are everywhere, probably formed by the vortexing into the center, as explained by Walter Russell. Matter will disintegrate by vortexing out (radiation), which is not part of the standard definition of black holes. Russell's concept of how matter cycles and disintegrates is a more likely scenario than a black hole that never disintegrates.

The pattern is the same as we move from the micro to the macro size (e.g., from atoms to galaxies).

Haramein, working with Dr. Elizabeth Rauscher, an American physicist, authored a series of papers that lay out a very compelling case for the torus as the shape of the fundamental patterning at all scales. In fact, the math indicated that the double torus is the basis of creating matter. This is reminiscent of the work of Walter Russell as well as Charles Leadbeater and Annie Besant. The content below is derived from Haramein's film, *Crossing the Event Horizon: Rise to the Equation*.

Sacred Geometry

Within the structure of the torus are also the elements of sacred geometry. At the core of the torus is a structure called the vector equilibrium (VE), or cuboctahedron. VE is a symmetrical array of eight tetrahedrons, with their bases representing the triangular faces of the VE, and all pointing towards the VE's center point. (The square faces are the bases of half-octahedra, like the form of the pyramids in Egypt.)

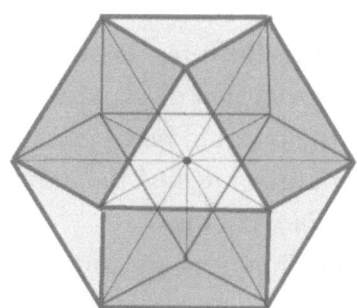

FIGURE 10. Vector Equilibrium (VE), or cuboctahedron

It is the only geometric form that has equal-length edges and radial vectors to its center point. A prime characteristic of the vector equilibrium is its ability to dynamically pulse in both left- and right-handed rotation from its fully expanded state (the VE structure) to its fully contracted state (an octahedron—eight faces, twelve edges, and six vertices), passing through a specific phase that creates an icosahedron (20 faces, 30 edges and 12 vertices; all faces are made of a triangle) as it does so.

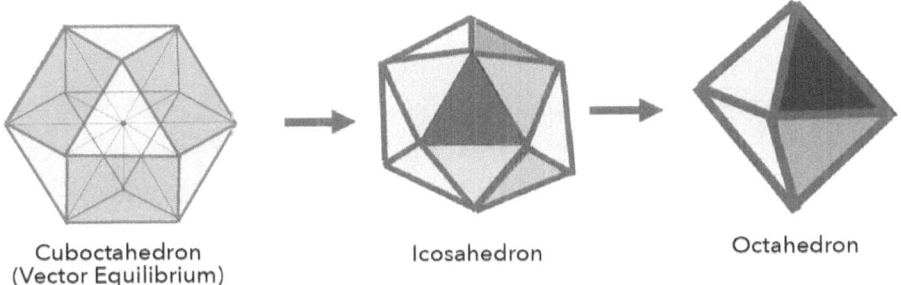

Cuboctahedron (Vector Equilibrium)   Icosahedron   Octahedron

Twisting Motion Changes Cuboctahedron to Icosahedron
Which Can Twist and Collapse to an Octahedron

FIGURE 11. Cuboctahedron—Icosahedron—Octahedron

Working to the next level of complexity of the VE, Nassim Haramein determined that if there were 32 positive (upward-pointing) and 32 negative (downward-pointing) tetrahedrons, for a total of 64 tetrahedrons, they then created the most balanced symmetry of positive and negative polarity. This formed the Isotropic Vector Equilibrium. The geometry consists of equal vectors and equal 60° angles. One can extend this equilibrium array infinitely outward from the center point of the VE, producing an Isotropic Vector Matrix (IVM). *Isotropic* means "all the same," *Vector* means "line of energy," and *Matrix* means "a pattern of lines of energy."

FIGURE 12. Isotropic Vector Matrix (IVM)

This can be seen as the infinitely-present-at-all-scales-and-in-perfect-equilibrium geometry of the zero-point energy field. Every point in this matrix is a potential center point of a VE, around which a condition of dynamic fluctuation may arise to manifest. VE geometry is inherent in this matrix.

The first *fractal* (the underlying geometric unit that everything else is made of) of the IVM is the 64-tetrahedron grid—the Isotropic Vector Equilibrium. The quantity of 64 is found in numerous fundamental systems. For example:

- 64 *codons* in our DNA code. A codon is three bases of the nucleic acids in DNA. Each codon codes for an amino acid. The condons code for all amino acids found in all proteins, which are the building blocks of matter in nature.
- 64 hexagrams in the I Ching. The Chinese used the I Ching to predict what happens, because things don't happen by chance. It forms a pattern, which gives information.

The number 64 is special in many ways. An example is that 64 is the first whole number that is both a perfect square and a perfect cube.

The Energy Flow of the Torus, Light Waves, and the Energy of Creation/De-creation

One characteristic of the torus energy flow is that there is a still point at the center of the central vertical axis of rotation. The torus both receives and emits energy simultaneously. It is self-sustaining and made from the medium in which it exists. We might also consider that the pulsing, pumping dynamic of the VE creates a toroidal flow.

Walter Russell's books talk about the spiraling compression of light to create the essence of the appearance of matter. The above discussion reveals that the vortices are structured in the form of a torus. All motion of the divided light passes through the center, with centripetal compression for creation and centrifugal expansion for disintegration. Russell also discusses the analogy of the male and female polarities (light) being the two ends of a lever (seesaw), being centered by God.

In *The Message of the Divine Iliad*, Russell says:

Behold thou the unity of all things in Light of Me, and the seeming separateness of all things in the two lights of my divided thinking. See thou that I, the Undivided, Unchanging One, am within all divided things, centering them, and I am without all changing things, controlling them.

If we see the light as waves, then the center is the still point of the wave from which changes occur. God is, asserts Russell, the "fulcrum of every wave of motion in the universe." The physical universe is created from the motion of the polarized light, which is centered/controlled by God. (From the torus perspective, the center is the center of the torus.)

Russell's definition of creation is:

All form is generated from the One source of thinking Mind by a preponderance of the concentrative pressures of the centripetal force of thinking.

De-creation (disintegration) is then defined as:

All form is radiated back into the One source of thinking Mind by a preponderance of the decentrative, expansive pressures of the centrifugal force of thinking.

In other words, nothing is destroyed; everything is a cycle of creation / de-creation for the physical universe. The One source of thinking Mind is separate from the cycle, but is the center of the process.

Summary of Key Points in This Chapter

Although complex thoughts are presented in this chapter, understanding the formation/creation of matter involves only a few key points:

- All matter formation is based on the spiraling (vortex) motion of light toward the center. Matter breaks down in the reverse spiral from the center.
- Spiraling motion can be viewed as torus.
- This is an endless cycle.
- The vortex or spiraling motion occurs in the dense, fluid-like medium called the *aether* (now often called the *quantum fluid*).

- All matter means everything physical — from atoms, to rocks, to plants, to animals, to suns, to galaxies.
- The forces pulling toward the center can be viewed as *gravitational.*
- The forces pushing out from the center can be viewed as *magnetic repulsion.*
- Such repulsive forces likely form the basis of why matter feels "solid." Quantum physics really teaches us that "matter" is really mostly empty "space."
- Since all matter is the "same" in terms of being motion/waves/fields, and since all are centered by God/consciousness, this forms the basis of the statement, "As above, so below."
- We can then postulate that the *centering quality* may be the basis of consciousness.
- Thus, everything from an atom to a rock to living organisms is "alive" based on their consciousness. (Obviously, there are different levels of consciousness — a rock or atom is different from a complex organism such as a human being or a plant.)

CHAPTER 5

How We Create from Our Thoughts

We are our thoughts.
We create our reality by how we perceive
our thoughts.

Most people do not give thoughts the consideration they deserve. Thoughts are generally considered the "stuff" that bounces around in our heads throughout the day. The left brain sometimes does work in trying to solve problems and analyzing situations. But our thoughts sometimes go into overdrive when we get angry at someone or some situation. If we are being attacked, our thoughts may go into the fear mode. But we seldom think that we create our reality from our thoughts.

By thoughts, I mean everything that is going on in the mind. In earlier chapters, we were reminded that the essence of our mind may not be in the "matter" of the brain. For people who have a near-death experience, out-of-body experience, or even are a hydrocephalic with mainly water in the areas of the brain, the "mind" is still there but not in the traditional concept of the brain. Since we have a body (which includes the brain), we will feel its influence — such as through our emotions; our hormones; the parts of the brain that have specific functions (e.g., the reptilian brain is associated with the "fight/flight/freeze" response); right-brain vs. left-brain ways of looking at reality; pain; joy; and so on. Our thoughts also will be influenced by many factors, such as our conditioning from parents, teachers, peers, society, etc.

Another way to talk about thoughts is to say, "We *are* our thoughts." We create our reality by how we perceive our thoughts. For example, if you get cut off in traffic by a driver, you can react by getting very angry, honking the horn, yelling at the driver, and remaining angry for the whole day — which influences everything you do that day. Or you can think, "That driver really needs to get to his destination — hope he gets there safely," and proceed to have a very nice day. You can thus create two widely different realities simply by what thoughts you hold.

By "reality," I mean our personal reality. It is our *personal* reality that we create with our thoughts. This is not the same as our *collective* reality, a reality that we all agree on. The collective reality is an implicitly agreed-on standard; it gives us a framework. It's what allows us to say, "This animal is a dog," or "That is a red flower," or "The sky is blue," or "This structure is a house."

Personal reality is quite different, and subjective in terms of yourself. One person who has many tasks can do them without feeling any stress, whereas another person in the same situation can be completely stressed out. One husband whose wife tells him "Make a right turn ahead" while he's driving can become angry because he feels that she keeps telling him how to drive, while another husband in the same circumstance instead would say, "Thank you for alerting me." It's all in how we see things, and consequently respond to them. Such experiences form the basis of our thoughts.

Our thoughts can be the basis of many of our emotions — whether happiness, love, anger, fear, joy, or anything else. We *are* our thoughts, and we can choose what those thoughts are. If you realize that we are all One and connected, then if you get angry, you realize that you are getting angry with a version of yourself.

The influence of our thoughts on our personal reality includes even the level of the physical body. Negative thoughts held over many years can manifest as a disease. A depressed immune system can allow infections or other diseases to come into being. The cause may be stress, but the stress itself may be caused by how we *think* about any situation. A wife who thinks about her husband, "You do not love me like other husbands love *their* wives" will often return to some version of this thought again and again. Over many years, her resentment towards her husband eventually may manifest as an ulcer, a tumor, or some other disease.

Our thoughts also influence our personal reality in terms of the state of our interactions with other people. One person can be prejudice-free and have trusting relationships with people who look different, while another person can feel that people with a different color skin cannot be trusted. Thus, how we perceive and think about things really creates our reality and how we live within that reality.

We are creating at every moment, but we often fail to realize it. At the level of collective consciousness, we actually are creating our environment. As a collective group, we are part of creating everything we see, smell, feel, hear, and taste. It is the *collective* that determines that this wavelength is defined as the color red, this smell is defined as the smell of a rose, this sound indicates that someone is at the door, this enclosure is defined as a house, etc.

On a more personal level, we are creating with our every thought. If we have fear, we often manifest what we fear. If you have a fear of a disease and continually think about the disease, you are bringing that disease into your reality—and you may get that disease. In healing, the practice is often not to give a label to a disease, but to just talk about a certain discomfort. Giving the disease a name gives it greater reality, along with the reality that is commonly accepted for that disease. If we have anger—especially if it is chronic—we may manifest a disease that corresponds with that frame of mind. If we concentrate on some pain we have and talk about it continuously, we then become *friends* with the pain, and so it does not go away. In contrast, if we concentrate on the success of our healing (or a project), then we will manifest the successful completion of that project.

Creating a Desired Reality

The *Law of Attraction* works on the basis of creation. We visualize what it is that we want to see or be, and then the Universe works with us to create our visualizations and manifest them as our experience of reality. Stated in terms of quantum physics, we create by "collapsing the wave." The observer (i.e., us) creates the outcome, based on how the experiment is designed (recall the double-slit experiments discussed in Chapter 3).

There are ways to activate relevant portions of the mind to bring about the inner state where this creation can come about. In Chapter 12, we'll discuss activation of the auditory portion of the brain, and how we can suddenly bring quiet into the midst of noise. And we'll discuss activation of the visual cortex, and how we can neutralize harmful electromagnetic radiation coming from electrical light sources that we see.

Caroline Cory, a visionary author and the founder of the OMnium Method of Learning and Healing (I learned much about who I am and the nature of reality from her Master's Course), introduced me to the "Human Creative Formula" in her book, *The Visible and Invisible Worlds of God*. In recent years, she has created some excellent documentaries, including the award-winning "Superhuman: The Invisible Made Visible." She explains:

> Not unlike your Divine Creators, you create through Thought. However, your thoughts are subject to your physicality and will materialize according to the following formula:
>
> **Human Creation = Thought + Desire + Belief + Surrender**
>
> THOUGHT is the asking, the conscious choice and focus of your intent.
> DESIRE is the impetus, the fuel or passion of your intent.
> BELIEF is the knowledge of self and faith in your potential.
> SURRENDER is your recognition as a Creator with the Divine order and your oneness with the Universal Forces which will assist you in the materialization of your intent.
>
> Thought, without desire, belief and surrender will not materialize. Desire without focused intent, belief or surrender will not materialize, for as you think, you must be assisted by cosmic forces and elementals who convert your thoughts into things. You are creators of reality. You cannot exist and create outside the Creator-Mind or without the divine beings and forces of the Universe.

Spiritual teacher and author Owen Waters, in *Spirituality Made Simple*, gives us a similar equation for creation. According to Owens, the equation for Universal Law of Creation is:

Creation = Thought + Feeling + Motion

As Owen puts it:

The only tool at the disposal of the Creator in making the universe was consciousness. Therefore, everything in the universe consists of consciousness — people, rocks, plants and planets — and because they consist of consciousness, they all have some degree of awareness. Creation was made possible when the Creator divided its consciousness into two complementary aspects — thought and feeling. It then intertwined these aspects and set them into motion in ways that were needed to develop life as we know it.

The universe, you, and everything around you consist of 100% consciousness. Life is but a dream, and each one of us is here to change the dream in our own unique way. Recreate your dream to realize all of your potential using the Universal Law of Creation.

Summary of Key Points in This Chapter

In this chapter, we learned that we *are* our thoughts.

- The essence of our mind/consciousness is *not* the body/brain—as evidenced by out-of-body experience, near-death experience, and the hydrocephalus condition.
- What we experience, sense, and feel are filtered though our thoughts. It is our thoughts that create anger, rage, resentment, joy, love, happiness.
- We learned that if we harbor negative thoughts for extended periods, the thoughts can manifest in diseases of the body.
- We learned the secrets of creation from Caroline Cory and Owen Waters:

Human Creation = Thought + Desire + Belief + Surrender

Creation = Thought + Feeling + Motion

CHAPTER 6

I AM

*We are all the thought creation of God
and thus a part of God.
And through that divine connection,
we are all connected and part of the One.*

Now we are ready for "I AM."
In the previous chapters, we have discussed my journey from spoon-bending and dowsing to encountering Joachim Wippich and his teachings (Chapter 1), Joachim's central message about healing and remembrance (Chapter 2), how you are not just your body (Chapter 3), the formation of matter (Chapter 4), and how we create from thoughts (Chapter 5).

So by this point, we can understand that we are eternal beings, and not the "matter" of our bodies.

We have also learned that the creation of matter is derived from the dynamics of the torus structure, vortex movement, and the resulting geometries. We have also learned that all matter is "centered" by a balancing condition, which we can call "God," or "Source," or "Consciousness." Walter Russell, in discussing creation in Chapter 4, says that God is centering all things. God is not matter but rather is that which *centers* matter.

In essence, everything we see is of God. That is, everything has a form of consciousness. Humans have a higher degree of consciousness, in that we are more aware than the vegetal and mineral worlds. It is this consciousness that enables a human being to communicate with plants (see the discussion of Cleve Backster's experiments in Chapter 3).

This same consciousness enables us to communicate even with stones. Robert Gilbert, of the Vesica Institute for Holistic Studies, has created new methods of vibrationally testing stones to determine their energetic powers and applications. In his seminars, students work with healing stones by learning to "listen" to their consciousness.

We are spirit, and the essence of our spirit is God. God made everyone in His own image. That is the basis of the statement, "We are all ONE." There is only God. And to help us understand this statement further, we are all the *thought creation of God* and thus a part of God. And through that divine connection, we are all connected and part of the One.

I AM Links Us to Our True Nature as God's Thought Creation

We are given free will. We are given the ability to be creators. We are not separate from God. The journey is to come back to the understanding that we are One with God and One with all of creation, One with all of humanity.

The concept of I AM now becomes clear. I AM links us to our true nature — a part of God as God's thought creation. Everyone is One with God. Everyone is I AM. Christ said, "God and I are One." According to His teachings, the goal is for people to reach the same conclusion — that every individual is One with God. In the *Course of Miracles*, the key message throughout its many pages is that the greatest sin is the belief in separation from God. Everyone is of Divine lineage.

Remember the wave analogy of who we are, from Chapter 3? We are like a wave, rising above the ocean water. We may believe that we are separate from the ocean, but we are part of it. The wave represents the I AM and the ocean represents God, and we are part of God.

There Is No Intermediary between You and God

The I AM message is embedded in all the great religions. The great avatars of these religions and philosophies taught that there is no separation between you and God. The original teachings tried to empower the individual to understand that there is no intermediary between you and God.

Unfortunately, however, through the desire to control people over the ages, power was often given to the intermediaries and their organizations (e.g., priest and church). This has resulted in the belief in separation (and all the subsequent separation beliefs) between you and the Divine.

When power is given to others (whether to religions, governments, or others in positions of power) rather than people believing in their own Divine nature, the resulting behavior shows a lack of belief in the Self. Many of the ills of individuals, societies, and countries can be traced to this lack of belief in the Divine Self. In general, people impose limitations on themselves because they do not realize who they really are—I AM. Everyone has a Divine lineage. Everyone is "I AM."

Joachim Wippich taught me a very powerful affirmation: "I AM Everything I AM." There's a physical gesture that goes along with this: To harmonize my right brain and left brain with my heart, I hold out my arms, then bring my hands together and say, "I invite my right brain and my left brain to come together with my heart in harmony." Then I say, "I invite my left brain and my right brain to come together with my heart in harmony." When I do that, I'm in harmony. (For women, it would be the other way around: first the left brain, then the right brain. *See* Chapter 7 for more details.)

Then I state, "I AM Everything I AM." This immediately brings me into the I AM vibrational frequency. When I make the statement "I AM Everything," I know deep in my heart that I AM One with God, the ocean of All, and that I AM that individuated wave which is part of the ocean.

The following poem, "I am the I AM," is the gift of enlightened transpersonal therapist and author Dr. Frances Vaughan. After Frances passed from the earth, she and her friend Cynthia Spring co-authored the "Greater Reality" Series of books (Frances from the discarnate side, Cynthia from the incarnate side). Their second book in the series is *Seven Questions about the Greater Reality*. Frances' wonderful poem below—channeled through Cynthia's and my mutual friend, the amazing channeler Regina Ochoa—puts the I AM in proper perspective.

I AM THE I AM

I am Love.

I am Music.

I am Art.

I am Learned Beyond my UNDERSTANDING.

I am Divine.

I am Love.

I am God.

I am Leader.

I am Co-Creator.

I am Co-Creation.

I am Love.

I AM the I AM

I am Pure.

I am Essence.

I am of Everything.

I am Frequency.

I AM the I AM

I am the Air I breathe.

I am the Ground I walk.

I am the Voice I hear.

I am the Song I sing.

I AM the I AM

I am Love.

I am the Wind in the Universe.

I am the Stars in the Cosmos.

I am the Creator of Thoughts.

I AM

I am These Thoughts.

I am Love.

I AM the I AM

I am Harmony.

I am Balance.

I am the Fulcrum.

I am the Plane atop the fulcrum.

I am The Shift.

I am the Libra to My Thoughts.

I AM the I AM

I am Love.

I am Harmony.

I am the Heartbeat to my Thoughts.

I am the Drum to my Beat.

I am the Resonation to my Drum.

I am the Frequency of my Heartbeat to the Universe.

I am Love.

I am the I AM

Walk with ME.

Walk with ME.

Walk with ME.

In ME, you will Feel Love.

In ME, you will Feel Balance.

In ME, you will Feel the Heartbeat.

In ME, you will Feel the Creator.

In ME, you will Feel the Creation.

In ME

You FEEL Love.

In ME

You ARE LOVE.

In ME you will travel the I AM.

In ME, you will be the I AM.

In ME, you are the Creator.

In ME, you are Co-Creation.

In ME, you are Creation.

In ME, you are the I AM.

You are the I AM.

You are Love.

You are Limitless.

You are Infinity.

You are the Recorder of ALL created.

You are the Record of All to be created.

You and I are ONE.

We are Co-Created in the I AM.

You are Love.

I AM Love.

You ARE the I AM.

I am the I AM.

I AM THE CREATOR.

I AM CO-CREATION.

I AM CREATION.

I AM LOVE.

I AM THE I AM.

Summary of Key Points in This Chapter

- We are not our bodies.
- Our essence is I AM.
- The essence of everything is I AM.
- God/Source is the essence of everything.
- We are One with God and with everything and everyone.
- Everything has consciousness with varying degrees of awareness.
- The "I AM the I AM" really says it all.

CHAPTER 7

Harmony and Balance

All created things seek balance and harmony.

If people do not realize that their essence is I AM, they may become more prone to the idea of separation—to believing that they are not connected to Source and are not One with others. This type of thought process can lead people to behave as if only their own needs and opinions matter. This, in turn, negatively impacts their ability to find balance and harmony.

People who *know* that they are the I AM realize their connectivity to Source and to all others. They learn not to make judgments, and they listen to all arguments in order to find the balanced/harmonious solution to any problem. They realize that perspectives gained earlier in life may not necessarily be true; that only by listening and working with others can they get closer to a solution that works for everybody, even though it might not be ideal for the two sides. They realize that compassion, love, and forgiveness may be part of what's required in finding balance.

Achieving Health, Happiness, and Harmony

Thus, the equation for finding happiness and health involves bringing the physical imbalances of matter (cells, life-supporting structures/organs, etc.) into harmony/balance, as well as reaching their I AM vibrational essence. This is why Joachim stresses both Harmony *and* the I AM (rethinking and remembering who we are).

In Chapter 4, Walter Russell said that God is "within all divided things, centering them." And when we discuss BioGeometry in Chapter

9, we will learn that the center of everything is where we find the harmonizing quality of BG3 (the centering principle that has become the cornerstone of the science of BioGeometry). Thus, when we are at our essence of I AM, we *are* the centering quality of Harmony and Love. Being I AM means being One with God and all humanity, and being the centering quality of Harmony and Love. All humans test positive with the harmonizing quality of BG3; BG3 is inherent within us. When we are not centered, disharmony can occur.

Whenever there is disharmony, there must be an underlying reason. Sometimes differences in polarity may create the tensions that result in disharmony. The physical world has inherent polarity, since its construction is based on polarity. This is evident in Walter Russell's statement that light is made polar by being divided into blue and red (for female and male) before being compressed to form matter.

Polarity Seeks Balance

We see polarity everywhere. There are males and females. There is a left brain and a right brain. We are right-handed or left-handed. There is yin and yang. Even the fingers of our hands are yin or yang. If you know how to dowse, you can dowse to ask whether each finger is yin or yang. You will find that each finger changes polarity following the polarity of the previous one: if the first finger is yin, the next is yang, and the following finger is yin, etc. It's the same with the hand itself: if the back of the hand is yin, the palm of the hand would be yang, and the other hand would be just the opposite.

Molecules can have both polar and non-polar aspects. Table salt has a positive sodium and a negative chlorine, to form sodium chloride. DNA (deoxyribonucleic acid), the building blocks of our genes, forms sequences that code for the molecules that form our body. The sequences result from polarities of how oxygen, nitrogen, and hydrogen are attracted to each other because of their polarity (often called hydrogen bonding of four nucleotides found in DNA).

As these examples show, nature will always seek balance. Yin will be balanced by yang. A positive sodium ion will be balanced by a negative chloride ion to form table salt. The bases in DNA will align in a sequence that forms balance.

Imbalances within the cells of the body can occur through the influence of our thoughts or hormones. The resulting disharmony then would need to be brought back into harmony.

For physical imbalances in the body, you can say an affirmation to invite in harmony with disharmony. For example, if you have pain in the cells of the arm, you can say an affirmation to invite in harmony with disharmony in the arm. You then would follow this with an affirmation statement to bring you to the I AM vibrational level.

For imbalances in thought, you also would need to realize that that you are your thoughts, by using the affirmation, "I am my thoughts."

Another way to look at this is to think about a seesaw. In the middle of the seesaw is a fulcrum. From the metaphysical perspective, this is the "center" from which all things are balanced. So you can think of harmony as the state in which the seesaw is completely level and everything is in balance. That balance is the desired outcome. All created things seek balance/harmony. We can also define happiness, and even love, as a state of harmony and balance.

Imbalance/disharmony is part of living life on earth, because the very nature of polarity can result in imbalance/disharmony. Therefore, when disharmony occurs, we need to try to bring back a state of harmony.

This takes place in nature as a matter of course: where there is an imbalance, conditions will occur to bring balance back. Imbalances of the earth can be released by earth movements (volcanoes, earthquakes, storms, etc.). Imbalances in weather patterns can result in, for example, tornadoes; these will run their course in order to create balance. In the animal world, imbalances between predator and prey (where too many predators cause the dying off of prey/food) result in the starvation of the predators until equilibrium is reestablished.

In the human condition, perceived inequities in relationships among groups of people (including nations) and between individuals can result in divorces, lawsuits, murders, battles, wars, and other major problems.

In one way or another, the pendulum will shift back to a point of balance. The secret is to understand the principle of balance/harmony.

The Principle of Balance/Harmony

Due to imbalances (whether from polarity or from belief of separation rather than connectedness), disharmony/imbalances can occur. In the case of disharmony between individual human beings or among larger groups of human beings (e.g., nations), if it isn't possible to reach total agreement there is always a middle ground. In the place of that middle ground, although neither party is completely "happy," enough of their needs can be met to sufficiently satisfy them so that conflict is resolved and a state of relative happiness is achieved.

Another way to look at harmony is to examine our thoughts. As we discussed in Chapter 5, thoughts can cause disharmony. Negativity, anger, and fear—as well as incorrect perceptions of others based on such environmental factors as parental biases; educational, governmental, or religious biases; incorrect judgments of friends, spouses, neighbors, political parties, races, immigrants, etc.—can cause imbalances.

In light of the potential effects of thoughts, we need to realize that all people must take responsibility for their thoughts, since it is from their thoughts that they are creating their own disharmony. Joachim Wippich offers the following affirmation:

"I AM responsible for my thoughts 100% I AM."

Taking ownership of our thoughts helps us enter into harmony and the I AM state.

The practice of Ho'oponopono, a Hawaiian system of reconciliation and forgiveness, works well in just this sense to bring about harmony. The book *Zero Limits* by Joe Vitale tells a story about how Hawaiian therapist Ihaleakala Hew Len was able to miraculously heal an entire ward of criminally insane patients without even meeting them. Len used the Ho'oponopono prayer for healing by just repeating the phrases, "I love you" (love); "I'm sorry" (repentance); "Please forgive me" (forgiveness); and "Thank you" (gratitude) over and over again. This is based on Len's idea of 100 percent responsibility, not only for one's own actions but also for everyone's. By connecting to Oneness, the four statements he said to himself were able to heal the other people.

The concept is analogous to the teachings of love and forgiveness by Christ. These are keys to holding an enlightened view of: no judgment; compassion; forgiveness; and love. This view leads to harmony.

At the level in the human body where disease manifests, bringing harmony and balance in with the disharmony in the body results in miraculous healings. This will be discussed further in Chapter 10 on "Healing."

Joachim's Way of Bringing in Harmony

Joachim Wippich offers various affirmations in Chapter 11 that are designed to invite harmony in with the disharmony. In his affirmations, the word "disharmony" is always used along with the word "harmony." If you are trying to bring in harmony, that means there must be *dis*harmony; stating the presence of disharmony acknowledges that a correction is needed in order to bring in harmony.

Bringing Harmony into the Physical Body

For example, if there is a pain in the arm (as mentioned above), an affirmation might be:

"I invite the cells in my arm to come into harmony with its disharmony."

By saying that, the cells in the arm realize that there is disharmony and will self-correct by coming into harmony. Before that time, the cells may not have realized that they were causing the disharmony of the pain. Thus, the message to the cells in the arm must be very explicit in order for harmony to come about.

Bringing Harmony into the Mind

Joachim has an excellent way of bringing the mind into harmony. In Chapter 11 on "Affirmations," which includes a section on Harmonic Dowsing, Joachim explains how to bring the mind into harmony before dowsing. He first has the dowser invite the right brain and the left brain to come into harmony with the heart. When the dowser follows instructions in that affirmation, the dowser comes into harmony. This chapter provides a number of excellent affirmations for achieving harmony for a variety of situations/problems and for remembering that you are the I AM. BioGeometry, discussed in Chapter 9, offers another unique view of harmony.

And Chapter 8, "Dowsing, Harmony, and the Vibrational Level," describes principles of dowsing that use harmony, as well as reaching the I AM level for greatest accuracy in dowsing. We will discuss this subject next.

Summary of Key Points in This Chapter

- The key to achieving health and happiness is to bring in harmony/balance.
- Disharmony/imbalances can be caused by a number of factors and is inherent in matter. Matter is formed from opposing polarities of light whose motion can result in imbalances.
- Thoughts/mind can be in a state of imbalance, causing disharmony.
- Taking responsibility for thoughts, and inviting in harmony and use of affirmations, can result in harmony.
- The Ho'oponopono prayer for healing is very effective and is just repeating the phrases, "I love you" (love); "I'm sorry" (repentance); "Please forgive me" (forgiveness); and "Thank you" (gratitude).

CHAPTER 8

Dowsing, Harmony, and the Vibrational Level

Dowsing is a tool to tap into the subconscious, and an excellent tool for determining your vibrational level.

To manifest healing, it's important to reach the I AM vibrational level. We will explain what that means in this chapter, as well as going into more detail in Chapter 10, "Healing — Harmony and the Self (I AM)" and Chapter 11, "Affirmations." In this chapter we will also discuss dowsing (both mental and vibratory), pendulums, and harmony.

Our Vibrational Level

When we are ill, angry, feeling disconnected, and lacking energy, we sometimes say, "My vibrational level is low." This statement has a lot of meaning. It is not a metaphor for a feeling. Instead, *it is a statement of our vibratory level at that moment.*

When you are functioning at the ego level, going about thinking and doing your everyday activities, your vibrational level is at an ordinary level. But when you consciously think and realize that you are I AM, your vibrational level goes up. This phenomenon is measurable and visually observable, if you know how to check this through dowsing.

Experienced dowsers often understand the statement "My vibrational level is low," since they often dowse to find out their vibratory level. They know that if they are not in balance and their vibratory levels are low, their ability to dowse accurately may be reduced. If their vibratory levels are high, the dowsing accuracy goes up.

Let me spend a few moments discussing dowsing, since this may be a new field for you.

Dowsing Works with the Subconscious

Dowsing is a tool to tap into the subconscious. Although you may use an external tool, such as a pendulum or L-rod, the truth is that *you* are the tool. It is *your* subconscious, by means of the right brain, that is directing the findings of the external tool. Whether it is a string with a weight at the end of it (a pendulum) or an L-shaped rod inserted into a hollow tube (an L-rod), its findings reflect your subconscious mind.

Early Applications of Dowsing

The field of dowsing has existed for many thousands of years. The most common early application of dowsing was in finding water. While this might seem mysterious or even far-fetched, if you think about it, this makes a lot of sense. After all, we *are* mostly water: in the adult human body, up to 60 percent. Since water is such a large part of our own makeup, our subconscious inherently knows the location of water underground. When a person dowses for water, the pendulum or L-rod will move to indicate the presence of water, even when that water is deep in the ground.

Another early use of dowsing was to find out which locations were optimal for building the great cathedrals of the world, and for ancient town-planning. This had to do with the locations of Ley Lines, which connected sacred power spots (usually known for their healing properties). There are subtle Earth-energy grids, the best known of which are the Hartmann Grid Lines (these run North-South and East-West) and the Curry Grid Lines (these run diagonal to the Hartmann Grid Lines). These Grid Lines can carry energy that is beneficial or harmful. If linked to the Ley Lines, the Grid Lines can carry harmonizing energies to buildings and other structures on these lines. The dowsing principles used in radiesthesia, or vibratory dowsing, can detect Hartmann and

Curry Grid Lines; and when they are made beneficial, they can detect the beneficial energies.

However, the applications of dowsing go far beyond only finding water and Grid Lines. Dowsing today has many applications—including healing.

Dowsing to Determine Your Vibrational Level

Dowsing is an excellent tool for determining your vibrational level. The speed of rotation of the dowsing tool reflects the level of your current vibration. When your vibrational level is high (at the I AM level), the pendulum or L-rod will spin rapidly. Whenever your vibrational level is sub-optimal, the spin speed will reflect that vibrational level and turn more slowly.

If your vibration is low—what then? The basis for achieving a high vibrational level is to remember and recognize who you really are — that you are *I AM*. When you are at your I AM level, then the pendulum or L-rod automatically spins rapidly. (We will go into raising your vibrational level later in this chapter, as well as in Chapter 11, "Affirmations.")

Many beginning dowsers sometimes have a problem getting the pendulum or L-rod to spin or move. There are usually two types of problems:

1. The first problem is that whenever you dowse with a pendulum or initiate a spin with an L-rod, you first need to initiate a 45-degree forward-and-backward movement of the dowsing tool in order to overcome its inertia.
2. The second problem occurs when energy is not flowing from your brain to the fingers of the hand holding the pendulum or L-rod. Joachim Wippich has found that first bringing your mind into harmony allows/facilitates the energy flow from the brain to the fingers of your hand to make your dowsing tool respond properly.

Anytime I want to bring in harmony, I hold out my arms. Then I bring them together and say:

"I invite my right brain and left brain to come together with my heart in harmony."

Then I bring my arms out and pull them together again, as I say:

"I invite my left brain and right brain to come together with my heart in harmony."

(This is the order for men; women would say it in the opposite order: first left brain/right brain, then right brain/left brain.) When I do that, I am now in harmony and the dowsing tool works well.

Following the harmony affirmation, I often state another affirmation to bring me to the I AM vibrational level. I use:

"I AM Everything I AM [here, I state my full birth name]."

Then the pendulum or L-rod really starts taking off, spinning rapidly, because now one is in the I AM state as well as in harmony. When I state, "I AM Everything," I know that I AM a wave in the ocean that is Divine Source. For me, the phrase puts into focus the connection that I, and everyone else, has with Divine Source. We are all part of the ocean that is Divine Source. Divine Source is Everything and we are part of Everything. In the Affirmations chapter, there are a number of different excellent Affirmations for reaching the I AM level of vibration.

(It is not standard practice, in the world of dowsing or radiesthesia, to do Harmony Dowsing and bring yourself to the I AM level. This is something that Joachim Wippich has taught. However, I find it so useful and practical that I use the Harmony Affirmation and I AM Affirmation for anything I do in terms of dowsing and radiesthesia.)

You can use the techniques of dowsing to make your vibrational states visible. Anyone can learn the steps.

But first, it helps to know the difference between standard (mental) dowsing, and vibrational dowsing (radiesthesia).

Mental Dowsing vs. Vibrational Dowsing (Radiesthesia)

These are the two kinds of dowsing you need to know about:

1. *Standard dowsing*, sometimes called *mental dowsing*. This is the form taught in all the chapters and clubs for dowsing. A dowser would just say that he/she is a dowser, and not use the term "standard" or even the term "mental." I am using the term to distinguish it from radiesthesia.
2. *Physical radiesthesia*, sometimes called *vibrational radiesthesia*. Often, those who practice radiesthesia do not even associate the term "dowsing" with radiesthesia, even though both practices make use of a pendulum but in quite different ways.

Standard, or Mental, Dowsing

Mental dowsing depends on constructs in your mind. You are mentally asking a question or making a statement. There is something at work in your mind behind this asking, whether you pose it as a question or a statement.

Because you really want to know the truth when dowsing, you don't want your mental expectations or desires to give you an answer. You want to tap into the much bigger database of the right brain to give you an unbiased answer. That is really the purpose of dowsing. When you are in harmony and at the I AM state, the right brain can answer without getting a biased answer from the left brain.

It is a *question* if you're asking someone, for example, "Is your name Mary Jane?" In this case, you would be dowsing to get a "yes" or a "no" answer. An example of a *statement* would be, "I am Mary Jane." In this case, you would be dowsing to verify the truth or falseness of the statement, and you are still dowsing for a "yes" or "no" answer.

The Right Brain Runs the Show

In mental dowsing, you can use both questions and statements. But how you state them is crucial, because answers are coming from the right brain, and you're not aware of it.

The right brain is extremely literal, lacking the left brain's analytical abilities, so it will take whatever you say as "That's the way it is" and answer accordingly. If what you say is not what you actually meant, well, you're going to get a wrong answer.

If you give the right brain a *specific* statement, it will listen and respond to that specific statement. For example, "This is a dog," or "This is a wolf," or "Do you know the difference between a dog and a wolf, yes or no?" In contrast, a question or statement that's very non-specific—something that's subject to interpretation, might be, "If Janet wins the election, will Janet endorse Edith to replace her?" The answer you get from the dowsing tool may not mean anything.

When you can ask questions in ways that that the right brain can't answer, the pendulum therefore can't answer in any helpful way. Or you might ask questions without sufficient specificity, and so a wrong answer can occur.

Being in the state of harmony and being at the I AM level helps prevent wrong answers that are caused when the left brain hijacks the dowsing to give you an answer that *it* wanted. You don't want answers from the left brain. You are really seeking answers from the right brain.

Why the right brain? Because it is said to have access to much more information than the left brain. The left brain, by not being burdened with almost unlimited information, can deal with specific information to make analytical decisions. The left brain does not have to know, for example, if there is water in the ground that can be accessed by digging a well that is 30 feet deep. The left brain may not know the location of a friend's lost key to the car.

The right brain, however, has all those answers, if the questions are asked in a specific way by the dowser. The right brain knows the size of a person's energy field (found by using a dowsing rod, which will open up upon reaching the edge of the person's field). Some people may say that the information is from the subconscious; I am using the terms "right brain" and "subconscious" interchangeably as the source of unlimited information that is hidden from the left brain.

Using a Pendulum for Mental Dowsing

For mental dowsing, any combination of string and a weight will work as a pendulum. These are easy to purchase, whether on the web or from various retail stores. Your local dowsing organization also will have them for sale. In the United States, the main organization is the American Society of Dowsers (ASD): *https://dowsers.org*. ASD lists chapters of the organization located throughout the United States.

This section discusses using a pendulum (whether store-bought or homemade) for *mental* dowsing.[1]

Later in this chapter, you will learn how you can make your own pendulum with some flour, salt, water, and a string ("Recipe for making your own neutral pendulum"). This homemade neutral pendulum can be used both for mental dowsing and radiesthesia dowsing. (We will get into radiesthesia dowsing in a later section of this chapter: "Using a Neutral Pendulum for Vibratory Dowsing.")

I first learned to dowse with a self-made pendulum using a string tied to a nut, as shown below.

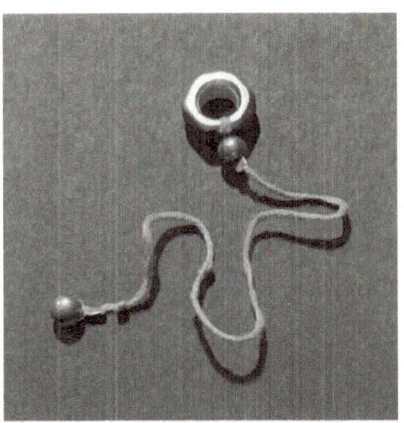

FIGURE 13. Homemade pendulum using a string and a nut

Steps to Mental Dowsing

A favorite book used for teaching about dowsing by the American Society of Dowsers (ASD) is Walt Woods' *Letter to Robin*, which describes mental dowsing. Woods describes the following dowsing steps:

> Hold the pendulum as shown, with the string between the thumb and index finger.

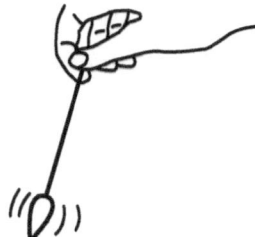

FIGURE 14. Pendulum held for dowsing

Now read the following six steps all the way through. This is just so you will have an idea of what you will be doing. You don't need to study them, just become familiar with them. Then come back and seriously go through them one step at a time. Ready? All set? Here we go:

Step 1. Relax, become quiet and drift into a prayerful mood *(alpha state)*.

Step 2. Take your pendulum *(any pendulum will do)* and hold the string or chain between your thumb and first finger. Hold it with about 11/2 to 3 inches string length. The string length will determine how fast it will swing. Next, hold the pendulum over the center of the chart.

Step 3. Now, manually *(by moving your hand and fingers)* make the pendulum start swinging towards the "YES" and ask and expect it to keep swinging on its own without your help. Ask it out loud, with about the same normal speaking voice and tone as talking to a person. If it stops, start it over again, ask it to keep going. Watch only the upper or forward half of the pendulum's swing and ignore the other half, from the center towards you. Repeat until the pendulum keeps swing on its own. You will be deliberately starting the pendulum and asking it to keep swinging with no additional help from you. You are simply training your system to react in a predetermined way.

Step 4. Do the same thing for the "NO." Your fingers are still over the center of the circle and you are ignoring one half of the swing.

Step 5. Once it is swinging by itself to the "NO," ask it, while it is still swinging, to work its way clockwise back to "YES" and then continue to the "Ready for Question."

Step 6. Next ask it to work its way counter-clockwise from the "Ready for Question" to "YES" and to the "NO," and then clockwise back to the "YES." Practice Steps 3, 4, 5 and 6 several times.

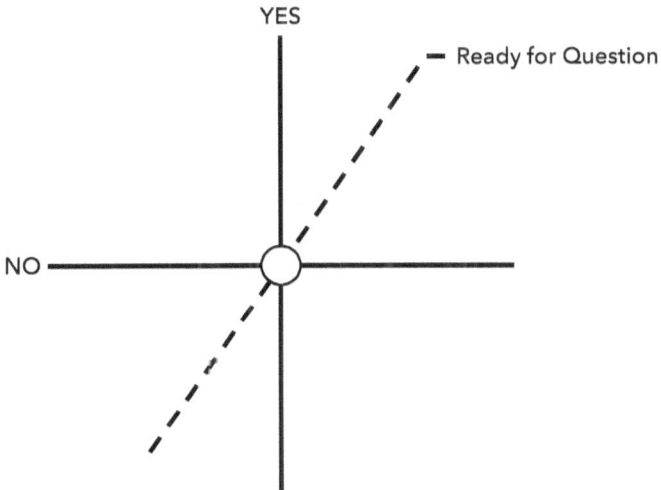

FIGURE 15. Directional guide for using a pendulum

This is just a sampling from Woods' booklet, *Letter to Robin*. To go into the subject more deeply, you can get the full booklet and follow its directions. An additional way to expand your understanding is to go to your local dowsing club or dowsing chapter (American Society of Dowsers/ASD) and learn from the experts.

Charting the "Yes" / "No" Movement

Dowsing requires training your muscles and memories to make the pendulum move in the 45-degree start motion, and the "Yes" and "No" directions. Once you are conditioned to make these movements, they will occur automatically when questions are asked.

In dowsing, you normally start the swing in the direction on the chart that says, "Ready for Question" (see above). This overcomes the pendulum's initial inertia, since it is already swinging. Then, when the question is asked, the pendulum moves to the "Yes" or "No" position. Once you are used to dowsing, you can use charts that can give you percent answers.

Three Questions for Dowsing Accuracy

Dowsing can be accurate, or it can be strongly influenced by your conscious mind. If you *want* a "Yes" or a "No," then when you dowse, the answer *will* be a "Yes" or "No." Joachim Wippich teaches an exceptional way to obtain the true answer. If you are in harmony and at your I AM vibrational frequency, your dowsing will be accurate. (See "Viewing Your Vibrational Level" later in this chapter.) Joachim does not ask questions but makes statements, which is different from traditional dowsing practices.

Walt Woods and other dowsers teach that, before dowsing, you should ask three questions: "May I, Can I, Should I?"

1. "May I?" means: Do I have appropriate permission to proceed and be involved?
2. "Can I?" means: Do I have the ability to successfully dowse in this area, and am I ready?
3. "Should I?" means: Considering all aspects related to this situation, would it be appropriate, proper, and suitable to dowse in this area?

Joachim has found that if you are dowsing for someone and ask the three questions, sometimes you will get a "No." You then need to check whether *you* are in harmony. You also need to check if *the person you are dowsing for* is in harmony.

To check this, have the person repeat the same harmony affirmation you used, and check to see if they are in harmony. Also have the person repeat one of the I AM affirmations. Invite the person to say the Rethink Affirmation:

"I AM Rethinking — Rethink I AM."

Saying the Harmony and Raising Vibrational Level Affirmation is also excellent to bring you or anyone you are dowsing for to the I AM level.

In most cases, if you follow the above steps, the "May I?" / "Can I?" / "Should I?" will become positive. If you are working on healing another person, very occasionally you may have to go beyond the physical level and address the emotional, mental, or spiritual levels to bring them into harmony.

(For further details, see the section on "Putting Yourself into Harmony" later in this chapter.)

Rules for Asking Questions

Walt Woods also has recommendations on asking dowsing questions. (Remember that you are speaking to your right brain, which takes your words literally.)

> **Rule #1:** You need to be very specific about what you want to know. This includes what, where, when, and sometimes instructional information relating to the question.
>
> **Rule #2:** Use only words, phrases, and conditions that you and the Dowsing System both agree upon their meaning, and for which there is an agreed-on method of dowsing response.
>
> **Rule #3:** Make the question a definite request for information that exists somewhere. Normally, don't ask for an opinion. If your question does involve an opinion of the past, present, or the future, it must be compared to an agreed-upon reference or conditions.

For beginners, a simple way to test your dowsing is simply make a statement: "My name is [state your name]." If this is true, the dowsing tool will give you a "yes." If you state a name that is not true, the dowsing tool will give you a "no" answer.

Vibrational Dowsing, or Radiesthesia

The difference between mental dowsing and vibrational dowsing (also called *physical radiesthesia* and *vibrational radiesthesia*) is that instead of mentally seeking an answer to a question, you are seeking *resonance* with an energy associated with whatever you are trying to measure. Radiesthesia uses resonance with energies at the level of awareness, rather than thinking about a subject and asking a question about it, which is the domain of mental dowsing.

In radiesthesia, the person uses the pendulum to find the resonant wavelength between the dowser and the object that is being measured.

I find radiesthesia techniques to have a high level of reliability, since it takes "thought" out of the method.

What Is Resonance?

Resonance is measured by a clockwise rotation of a pendulum, once you have found the wavelength of the vibration as determined by the length of the string.

To understand this, imagine a monochord instrument where a string is attached, such as a violin. (The dictionary defines a monochord as "an instrument for comparing musical pitches mathematically, using a taut wire whose vibrating length can be adjusted with a movable bridge," but this process also takes place with regular musical stringed instruments, such as a violin.)

When you pluck that single string, it will vibrate and sound as a certain pitch or note. The note created in this way has a wavelength to it, which defines that note.

The vibration of the string you have plucked will be in resonance with other strings that share a proportional string-length (e.g., example, twice as long, half as long; twice as short, half as short). And then they will all vibrate in multiples and octaves, ad infinitum.

So when you work with a pendulum, that wavelength is measured by the length of the string. You can use a pendulum and find the resonance of whatever it is that you're asking about. You can find the string length that is in resonance with practically anything—e.g., a color, a food, yourself, etc.

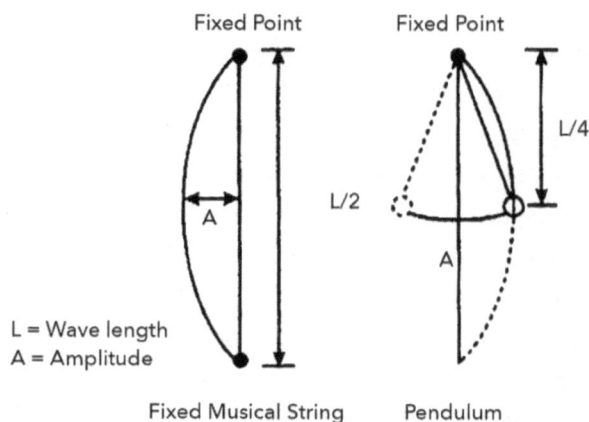

FIGURE 16. Resonance analogy

Finding the String Length of Your Personal Wavelength: You can find the string length of yourself (your personal wavelength) by checking the length that resonates with the back of your hand. You can then put your hand over a food or supplement to link yourself with that food or supplement. Using the string length of your personal wavelength can determine whether specific foods are in resonance with you, and thus tell you whether they're right for you. In essence, you are finding out if the food vibrates *in accordance with you* versus interfering with you.

What the Pendulum's Motion Indicates: If the pendulum is vibrating in a way as to indicate that this food is interfering with you, it will go counterclockwise. If that food won't make any difference for you, the pendulum will just go back and forth. But if that food is in resonance with you and will make you stronger—that is, if it's *good for you*—then the pendulum will go clockwise. (We discuss the movements of a pendulum and what they mean, below.)

So in light of what we said earlier about the wavelength of a vibrating string—how proportional string-lengths will vibrate, even if only a single string has been plucked—this musical analogy applies to how you can be in resonance (or not) with whatever it is you are asking about.

Tuning forks work exactly the same way. When you strike the tuning fork, all the other octaves will start vibrating. That's why the other tuning forks—which are twice, or half, or whatever proportion in relation to the fork that's been struck—will start vibrating, for exactly the same reason.

Between the two methods of dowsing—mental and radiesthesia—radiesthesia is inherently more accurate, since when resonance occurs you are looking at vibrational levels. Mental dowsing, in contrast, is more subject to the questioner's wish for a particular desired answer, which influences the pendulum to produce a "yes" answer or a "no" answer. However, if you first come into harmony with the left and right brain and the heart, and then bring yourself to the I AM vibrational frequency, then the pendulum's answer will be accurate.

You are seeking not "yes/no" answers but *resonance* between the dowser and what is being asked about. This is where wavelength comes in.

Using a Neutral Pendulum for Vibratory Dowsing (Radiesthesia)

One of the advantages of a neutral pendulum is that it will not resonate with other materials when used in radiesthesia testing—that is, it is *neutral*. I find radiesthesia techniques to have a high level of reliability, since they take the "thought" out of the method.

A neutral pendulum can be made of wood, acrylic, or another non-crystal material. Vesica Institute *(https://vesica.org)* sells neutral pendulums made of 1-inch acrylic balls with string. I have made neutral pendulums from self-hardening polymer clays, available at any craft store or online.

However, the least expensive way (and possibly the quickest) is to make one yourself out of flour and salt, as described below. This kind of pendulum works very well for the techniques described in this chapter. It is fairly light (a pendulum needs enough weight not to be totally weightless) and rotates well.

Recipe for making your own neutral pendulum from flour and salt:

The dough:
- Mix ¼ cup salt and ½ cup flour with a little less than ¼ cup of water. (This is a consistency that works for me.)
- Knead the dough.
- Take enough dough to form a form a 1-inch ball (or any other shape you want).
- Cut a string length of about 7 inches.
- Tie a knot on the end of the string and insert it into the dough. (The knot helps prevent the string from pulling out of the pendulum.)
- Then form the pendulum, keeping the string in the center of the ball of dough so that the pendulum is balanced. (You can also place the pendulum on some flour as a cushion to prevent it from deforming while drying.)

The string:

For string (typically sold as twine), #12 size is a good thickness. Don't get tar-coated string; it is too stiff. Nylon string is also problematic: it tends to unwind, so you have to coat the ends with glue. Most personal wavelengths run around 1.5 inches (that is, the length of the string that corresponds to your resonant energy), so for practical purposes you don't need an excessive string length.

Let the pendulum dry:

- Let the pendulum dry on its own for a few days.
- At that point, you can (if you want to) tie a loop at the end of the string and place the loop on your pinky finger so that the excess string doesn't get in the way. But since you don't need an excessive length (as mentioned above), this is optional.
- If you want to eliminate the rougher dough feel of the pendulum, you can give it a light coat of polyurethane (totally optional).

Below are a few pendulums I made using the above procedure.

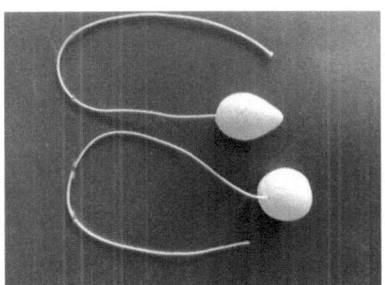

FIGURE 17. Pendulums made of salt, flour, water + string

The Neutral Pendulum and Your Personal Wavelength

A neutral pendulum is a pendulum with a neutral material—such as a plastic (e.g., acrylic) ball; wood or a weight made of flour, salt, and water (see above recipe)—attached to a string. All materials and electromagnetic energies—including the human body—are vibrating, and will thus resonate when they are at the wavelength that defines them. Remember our earlier analogy of a monochord instrument (a single-string instrument that can be plucked to generate a note) or a tuning fork? When any note on the string or tuning fork is played, octaves above or below the note of the monochord or tuning fork will vibrate. This is because they are in resonance with the primary note.

The length of the string on the pendulum is analogous to the wavelength of the note being plucked on the monochord instrument. When you hold the string of a pendulum where it meets the pendulum body, and you gradually release the pendulum body and thereby extend the length of the string above the back of your hand, *the string length at which the pendulum starts rotating clockwise is called your "personal wavelength."* As you slowly lower the pendulum body on the string, you initiate a 45-degree swing to overcome inertia. The 45-degree swing changes into a clockwise rotation when the personal wavelength string-length is reached (usually around 1.5 inches).

What this means is that the pendulum is now in resonance with your body. Anything that is good for your body will resonate positively (that is, the rotation will go clockwise). If something is not healthy for you, the pendulum will move in a counterclockwise direction. If something is neutral for you (neither good nor harmful for you), the pendulum will just move back and forth.

Once I know my personal wavelength, I can do simple tests with a neutral pendulum to know what is good for me. I can go to the grocery store and know which vegetables, eggs, meats, and fruits are good for me. I can tell which vitamins or supplements will be effective for me. If someone says that a particular essential oil will be beneficial for me, I can tell if that is true or not. I can tell if the microwave electromagnetic field of a smart meter or a cell phone will be detrimental to me. With a BioGeometry tool (*see* Chapter 9), I can make corrections and tell whether the corrections worked or did not work. All this can be done with a neutral pendulum and finding your personal wavelength.

The picture below shows examples of some neutral pendulums, one made of acrylic and the other of wood.

Dowsing, Harmony, and the Vibrational Level

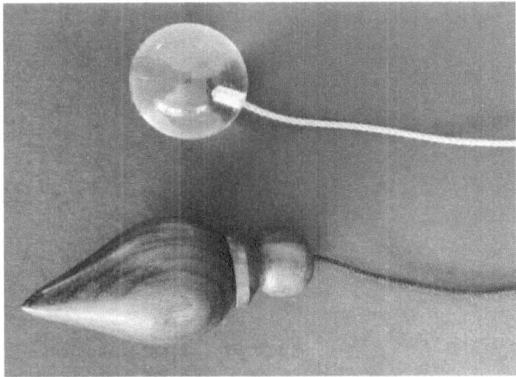

FIGURE 18. Pendulums made of acrylic (top) and wood (bottom)

The following photos show how to drop a pendulum along the string to find the length at which the pendulum rotates clockwise. This is your personal wavelength.

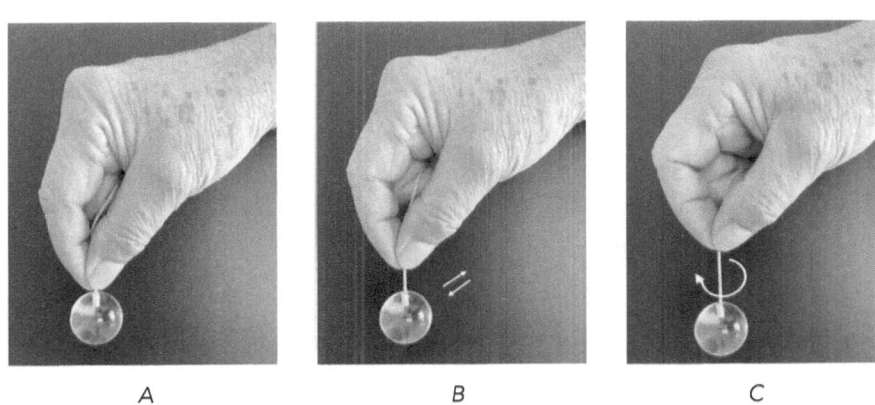

A B C

FIGURE 19. How to find a pendulum's clockwise-rotation length (personal wavelength)

(A) Hold the string next to the pendulum above the back of the hand

(B) Slowly releasing the pendulum on the string, move it back and forth above the back of the hand

(C) When string length reaches the resonant length, the pendulum will rotate in a clockwise manner above the back of the hand = the personal wavelength

Robert Gilbert, at the Vesica Institute, has an excellent instructional YouTube reviewing how to use a neutral pendulum: *https://youtu.be/rklULOn8p0w*.

One form of practice described by Robert Gilbert in this video is to hold the neutral pendulum over a battery. When you start the forward-and-backward motion of the pendulum, the pendulum will rotate clockwise over the positive pole and counterclockwise over the negative pole. A picture of this exercise is shown below.

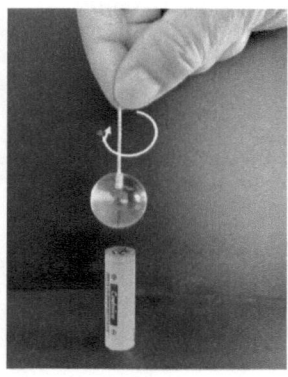

(D) For practice, when you hold the neutral pendulum above a battery and initiate the to-and-fro movement, the pendulum rotates clockwise over the positive pole and counterclockwise over the negative pole

A summary of finding your personal wavelength:

- Hold pendulum string between thumb and index finger at base of string and pendulum body.
- Hold pendulum above back of hand.
- Slowly release (lower) pendulum over back of hand while initiating a 45-degree swing to overcome inertia of a non-swinging pendulum.
- At around 1.5 inches, pendulum starts rotating clockwise as it finds the length of string corresponding to your personal wavelength.
- You can now check if you are in resonance with anything you want to test by holding, touching, or pointing to test object.
- Resonance indicated by clockwise spin, negative effect by counterclockwise spin, neutral by back-and-forth motion.

There is much more you can learn about the use of the neutral pendulum, if you are drawn to this subject. The BioGeometry Foundation

Course teaches the use of the neutral pendulum and personal wavelength technique, plus much more: *https://www.biogeometry.ca/home* and *https://vesica.org/*

Having a Neutral Mindset

It's not just the pendulum that needs to be neutral. *You* do as well. You have to be in a certain state of mind—a neutral awareness—when you're dowsing with the pendulum. When you ask a question, you're not thinking, "I want this pendulum to go clockwise" or "I want it to go counter-clockwise." You're just looking at something that the pendulum will give you information about, and being aware that you're looking at it and measuring its resonance energies. You're not thinking anything beyond that. You're just letting the energy of your body and your right brain come down through your hand and cause the pendulum to go clockwise, counterclockwise, or back and forth so that it's the *energy* doing it, not your conscious mind.

Rather than thinking, "I'm going to make this a mental dowsing exercise, and I want the pendulum to go clockwise," you need to wait a second or so to let that energy flow from your mind into the pendulum and move in the direction it should move. You have to let the pendulum do its thing; and the best way to do this is to be neutral, to be in a state of awareness without thought. You don't want to be thinking, "I need to make this thing turn." You're just getting the pendulum into motion, and it will turn on its own.

It's okay to think something on the order of, "I'm looking at this for the purpose of resonance," so that the right brain knows what to do. But you do want to get the mind out of the way.

That is, you *are* making things turn; but you're not doing it *consciously*, only *unconsciously* by means of the right brain. Where in mental dowsing you've already engaged your mind to get a "Yes/No," "True/False" answer, in vibratory or resonance dowsing you have to pull your mind way back and get into harmony with I AM. At that level, your right brain can do its thing and look at the truth.

Viewing Your Vibrational Level

You can check your vibrational level by means of a neutral pendulum.

The following exercise will help you practice the *rotational movement* of your pendulum or L-rod. Almost any pendulum or L-rod will work.

The best string length to use is the personal-wavelength distance (about 1.5 to 2 inches), although this does not have to be a personal-wavelength exercise. Thus, any pendulum will work. The point of the practice is to achieve an automatic clockwise rotation of the pendulum that reflects your vibrational level. Your mindset is to seek your vibrational level. You still overcome inertia by getting the pendulum to move at a 45-degree direction; and when your mind says "vibrational level," the pendulum starts to rotate clockwise.

If you are working with an L-rod rather than a pendulum, you would hold it upright, as shown in the picture below. Its rotation will be *counter*clockwise. The pendulum and L-rod are actually rotating in the same direction—it just depends on whether you are looking down (pendulum) or looking up (L-rod).

Once the body knows how to make a pendulum or L-rod rotate, it is, as we said, the energy of the subconscious or right brain that causes this to take place. You are not consciously trying to make the pendulum rotate. That is, it is still you moving the dowsing tool, but it is not moving based on your conscious intention.

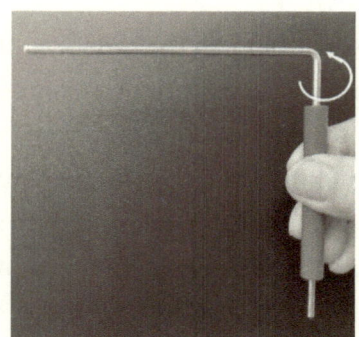

FIGURE 20. Holding the L-rod, with a counterclockwise rotation

However, you do need to make a physical movement to get things started. You always begin by initiating a forward-and-backward movement of the pendulum (or spin of the L-rod) to overcome the tool's inertia. Then the pendulum will have its own life in terms of its movement.

When your vibration is at the I AM level, the pendulum or L-rod spins rapidly, compared to a much slower spin when you are not connected to the I AM level.

Dowsing for Your Vibrational Level

There are a number of ways to check your vibrational level with a pendulum. You can ask the question, "Am I at my I AM vibrational level?" A "Yes" or "No" gives you some information. However, if you are at less than 100%—for instance, 25% or 50% or 80% of your optimal I AM vibrational level—then asking a simple question will not tell you your level.

What you *can* do is dowse in increments of 10% to get a number—for example, "Am I at 90%?"—then dowse. Repeat with each increment: "Am I at 80%?"—then dowse. Repeat until you get a "Yes."

You can also use a chart with percentages. You will be able to find a chart in Walt Woods' book, *Letter to Robin* (as well as almost any dowsing book or by checking with your dowsing organization).

I often write "0" to "100" on a piece of paper; this becomes my chart.

    0 10 20 30 40 50 60 70 80 90 100%

I then ask, "Show me my vibrational level as a percent on this chart."

You can do this by first moving the pendulum in the 45-degree position; the pendulum will then move to the correct percentage. (Hint: it's best to practice this technique with questions for which you know the answer.)

In addition to training your pendulum to show a percentage, you also can train it to move in a clockwise direction to indicate your vibrational level. When you are in resonance with yourself at your personal wavelength, the pendulum automatically spins clockwise. When you dowse for your vibrational level, you will use the clockwise motion to show your level of vibration. You will need to practice moving the pendulum in a clockwise motion before using it to show vibrational levels.

(Which is why you were invited to practice moving your pendulum in a clockwise rotation.)

The simplest way in which I normally check my vibrational level is to ask the pendulum, "Show me my vibrational level." Start the pendulum in a 45-degree motion and then let it rotate in a clockwise direction of its own accord. In this case, you are qualitatively using the rate of clockwise spin as an indicator of the vibrational level. You will learn from experience that when your right and left brain are not in harmony with your heart and you are not in the I AM vibrational state, the rate of clockwise spin is much slower. Being in the right brain/left brain/heart harmony allows the energy to flow to the hand/fingers holding the dowsing tool and make it function. When both harmony and the I AM state are working together, this significantly increases the rate of spin.

Putting Yourself into Harmony

For a pendulum to respond well and accurately, always start by putting yourself into a state of harmony. (Although this feature is not taught in regular dowsing, Joachim recommends this, and I have found it to be truly helpful.) As soon as you're in harmony, the dowsing tool will turn on its own.

At the minimum, repeat the first part of the words in the Harmonic Dowsing Affirmation (you'll find more on this in Chapter 11). To enhance the power of the following words, it is helpful to spread your hands out to the sides and then bring them together so that your palms meet, as you invite both sides of your brain to join together with your heart.[2] (Note that women and men do it in the opposite order.)

(For women):

"I invite my left brain and my right brain to join together with my heart. I invite my right brain and my left brain to join together with my heart I AM"

(For men):

"I invite my right brain and my left brain to join together with my heart. I invite my left brain and my right brain to join together with my heart I AM"

You do not necessarily need to be dowsing to bring in harmony between your brain and your heart. You can do this affirmation at any time, under any circumstance, to bring in balance and harmony.

Raising Your Vibrational Level

To bring yourself to the I AM level, you can use any of a number of affirmations. (*See* Chapter 11 for the full range.)

1. You can use the rest of the Harmony Dowsing Affirmation. Joachim states in that Affirmation:

> "I AM aware that all components of my divine being are active, present and functioning at 100%."

He explains:

> When I invite [people] to come to the place of perfect light, divine harmony and love, their readings turn to a "yes" every time. Their soul is now in harmony, far beyond the physical level. They dowse from the place of I AM.
>
> When I AM is said, it refers to the pure, loving essence of YOU: the divine individual God created to manifest your life on earth physically, spiritually and emotionally. As you refer to yourself in that way, you open up your heart and mind for divine inspiration.
>
> I AM means accepting myself. "I" alone does not indicate continuity, which is also the reason for putting I AM at the end of a phrase.

2. Or you can simply use the last part of the affirmation for "Harmony and Raising Vibrational Level to the I AM":

> "I AM Rethinking — Rethink I AM."

I AM is a difficult concept for most people to comprehend immediately. Thus, the need to "Rethink" the concept of I AM. The statement that Joachim commonly uses is: "I AM Rethinking — Rethink I AM." The process of "Rethinking—Rethink I AM" helps people to reach an understanding of the I AM concept.

Since most people do not realize who they really are, in order to raise their consciousness to the I AM level so that healing can occur, they must be asked to remember and "rethink" the concept of I AM:

"I AM Rethinking — Rethink I AM."

(Repeat this phrase 3 times.)
Reflect on this until you are at "I AM 100% I AM."
Then close with:

"I AM [full birth name] I AM."

3. A short, simple affirmation that works for me is:

"I AM Everything I AM."

Saying this makes the dowsing tool take off, because you are now in the I AM state. This concept was previously described in this chapter under the heading, "Dowsing to Determine Your Vibrational Level."

4. Another favorite affirmation statement that raises the vibrational level is:

"I AM 100% God's creation throughout my evolutionary thought-creation.

I AM [Full Birth Name] I AM"

You will notice a big difference in the rotation speed of your pendulum or L-rod after bringing yourself into harmony, and then a further jump when you bring yourself to the I AM level.

All these affirmations work. It's whatever brings you to the I AM level. When I AM is realized, your vibrational level goes up.

Summary of Key Points in This Chapter

- We learned that when we consciously bring ourselves to our I AM level, we experience an increase in our vibrational level.
- Our vibrational level can be measured and visualized through dowsing.
- Because of the importance of being at the I AM level, this chapter teaches fundamentals of dowsing.
- We learned about both standard mental dowsing as well as radiesthesia, where we dowse to detect subtle energies.
- Both methods are able to detect and measure our vibrational level.

- Radiesthesia also allows us to determine our personal wavelength, the wavelength that is in resonance with our personal energies. Knowing our personal wavelength gives us the ability to determine what foods and supplements are good for us (in resonance with us).
- We learned some affirmations that will raise our vibrational level to the I AM level.

Notes

[1] If you know nothing about personal wavelength and are just doing mental dowsing but you want to know your own vibrational level, you can use string lengths other than the personal wavelength and it will work. If you are using an L-rod, there is no string length involved; however, the rate of rotation still indicates the status of your vibrational energy.

[2] You do not necessarily need to be dowsing to bring in harmony with your brain and heart. You can do this at any time, under any circumstance, to bring in balance and harmony.

CHAPTER 9

Harmony and BioGeometry

BioGeometry is a way to bring about harmony into places, situations, and human experience.

BioGeometry is a way of detecting and generating energy qualities that have a harmonizing effect, and—if these energy qualities are not inherently present or are negative—providing a way of harmonizing those negative energy qualities so that they become beneficial rather than detrimental for us.

Harmony is important for healing to occur (we discuss healing in Chapter 10). And BioGeometry is a way to bring about harmony in places, situations, and human experience.

Detecting Subtle Energies for Locating Temples, Cathedrals...and More

Although BioGeometry is a present-day way to bring about harmony by means of a harmonizing subtle-energy quality, this science builds on the ancient tradition of being able to detect and work with powerful subtle energies.

Historically, sacred power spots were chosen as the basis for the construction of key structures such as temples and cathedrals. But did people know where the power spots were? How were these sites located?

We've already explored radiesthesia in Chapter 8. The ancient Egyptians were profoundly familiar with what we have come to call "radiesthesia." They used tools based on subtle energy to locate the sites for building sacred monuments. Then, in ancient Roman times, Augures (we would call them "dowsers" today) used specially calibrated staffs for city planning. Later, these same ancient skills for locating power spots for construction of sacred buildings were carried over by the Arabs and brought to Europe during the 15th-century Renaissance, to be used in the building of cathedrals. And the benefits of this kind of location weren't limited to locating sites for the purpose of building; the Jesuit monks used these same skills for finding beneficial herbal remedies.

In the 1950s, the French radiesthesia researchers Chaumery and Belizal[1] developed color scales and instruments to describe and detect those subtle energies that the ancient Egyptians, Romans, Arabs, and Europeans had made use of. They called their field *micro-vibrational physics*.

At the same time, German researchers such as Hartmann, Curry, and others[2] revived the detection of "Earth Energy Grids" and developed special tools to detect them.

BioGeometry and BG3

A significant outgrowth of this ancient knowledge is the science of *BioGeometry*, a new field developed by Dr. Ibrahim Karim and explained in his book, *Back to a Future for Mankind: BioGeometry*. The cornerstone of the science of BioGeometry is the "One Harmonizing Subtle Energy Quality," which he called *BioGeometry Three (BG3)*.

In Dr. Karim's words, BioGeometry Three (BG3) can be characterized as:

> The three basic qualities that are in resonance with The One Harmonizing Subtle Energy Quality and are used to detect it:
> 1. Horizontal Negative Green (this will be explained momentarily)
> 2. Higher Harmonic of Ultra Violet
> 3. Higher Harmonic of Gold
>
> They are found simultaneously as the main components of the One Energy Quality.

BG3 is found at sacred power spots and at the centers of structures (e.g., the center of a circle). BG3 has a harmonizing quality. Increasing BG3 can harmonize energies that are causing disharmony (e.g., electromagnetic fields). Bringing in BG3—which brings in harmony—is an important prerequisite for healing to occur. However, the addition of the three qualities will not in themselves produce the One Harmonizing Quality.

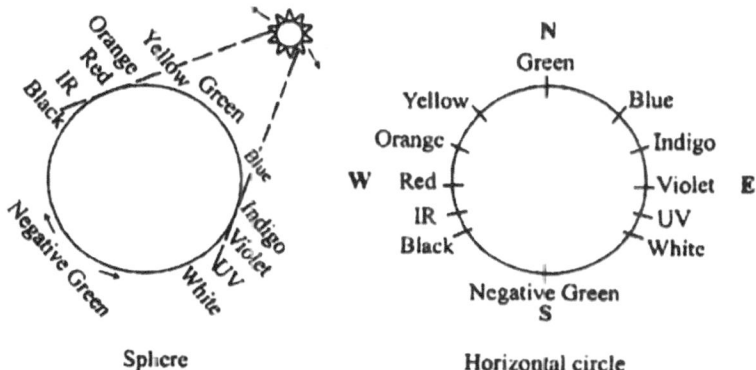

FIGURE 21. Colors found by resonance in a sphere facing the sun and on circle drawn on paper, with compass directions indicated

A Refresher on Resonance

To understand how BioGeometry works, let's dip back into the subject of resonance for a moment. (We discussed it at more length in Chapter 8.) Resonance is what takes place if you hold a vibrating tuning fork for the note C and another tuning fork also starts vibrating. Then you know that the other tuning fork is *in resonance with* the note C—just in a higher or lower octave than the original tuning fork.

To connect this with what happens in BioGeometry, we can use the neutral pendulum (described in Chapter 8 on dowsing) to find resonance of the energy qualities found with BG3. (The resonance-analogy with the wavelength of the note C, here, is the length of the string between your hand and the body of the pendulum.)

Finding Resonance with BG3

Using the string length, it's possible to use the neutral pendulum to find the resonance with the three energy qualities found in BG3: that is, gold, ultraviolet, and "horizontal negative green."

For detecting the higher harmonic of gold, one can use the neutral pendulum to come into resonance with gold. It turns out that gold is also in resonance with the colors orange and yellow, so one can substitute those colors to find the string length to be in resonance with gold.

For detecting the higher harmonic of ultraviolet, one can use ultraviolet light.

To understand and detect horizontal negative green, we first need to understand how colors express around a sphere.

Using a neutral pendulum and any sphere (e.g., a globe), hold the sphere outdoors in the presence of sunlight. Different positions on the sphere resonate with different colors—for example, there is a position on the sphere that is in alignment with the sun that resonates with the color green. In practice, you can find the string length on the pendulum that resonates with the color green. When you go around the sphere, that string length, representing wavelength, will be found at the alignment facing the sun (i.e., your neutral pendulum will rotate in a clockwise direction).

As an alternative to using a sphere, it was shown that a circle drawn on paper will resonate with the color green at the north direction. Resonance with the other colors are shown in the diagram below, both as a sphere and as a circle. As an added piece of information, if you had a neutral pendulum and no compass, all you would have to do to find direction would be to draw a circle on the ground. Once you found the position on the circle that resonates with the color green, you would have the direction North. The presence of red and violet would indicate West and East, respectively.

The string length (wavelength) of the neutral pendulum corresponding to the position opposite green is called "negative green." It has a penetrating power, since that energy penetrates through the sphere. All energies have a horizontal and a vertical aspect, which differ by slight differences in wavelength. For BG3, the energy quality that is found is the horizontal negative green wavelength. It turns out that horizontal subtle energies are beneficial, and vertical energies are detrimental to humans.

BioGeometry, Harmony, and Healing

Applying the principles of BioGeometry results in bringing harmony into an environment. Harmony and the I AM vibrational energies are fundamental for healing.

So if BG3 is present, there will be harmony. If something is causing disharmony in an environment, BioGeometry tools can be used to bring in harmony. (See the section in this chapter on "The Amazing Results of Bringing in Harmony through Increased BG3" for more about this.)

Dr. Karim designed several pendulums that resonate with BG3. These pendulums will rotate clockwise whenever BG3 is present. BG3 is the One Harmonizing Quality, not the three separate qualities used to detect it. You don't get BG3 by adding the three qualities used to detect BG3. The BG3 pendulum is in resonance with the One Harmonizing Quality, which is BG3. Thus, you do not need to measure the three energy qualities for detecting the presence of BG3.

In addition to harmony, BG3 is associated with the center. Another way to state this is that harmony is found in the center. If you draw a circle and test for the presence of BG3, you will find it in the center. If you draw an angle, then half the angle has the quality of BG3 (e.g., for a 90-degree, BG3 is located at 45 degrees).

The Amazing Results of Bringing in Harmony through Increased BG3

Dr. Karim discovered that when BG3 is present or its level is increased, there is a centering, harmonizing effect in the environment. An increase in BG3 quality can be achieved in a variety of ways, including using shapes, geometric structures, angles, colors, designs, locations of objects, colors, numbers (as units, not Arabic numerals), and sounds.

The real world causes all sorts of things to happen that can result in disharmony, e.g., negative frequencies from electromagnetic fields (EMFs), chemicals, pollutants, people acting out their frustrations in anger—all kinds of things that upset the balance/harmony.

An Example of a Swiss City Eliminating EMF Hypersensitivity

Certain *shapes* can augment BG3 qualities. Bringing such BG3 enhancing shapes into a place where microwave radiation (EMF) are affecting people (e.g., cell towers emitting EMFs) will harmonize the negative emissions and bring about protection.

In Switzerland, the residents of the cities of Hemberg, and later, Hirschberg, were complaining about the negative effects of the cell towers being placed in their towns. Many people, animals, and birds were being negatively affected by the microwave electromagnetic fields (EMF). Dr. Karim created certain geometric structures (e.g., the *Hemberg emitter*) and cubes with geometric designs to neutralize the effect of the EMF. He was so successful in getting rid of the hypersensitivity of Hemberg's people and animals to EMF that the city of Hirschberg also commissioned Dr. Karim to solve their problem, which he did.

An Example of the Use of BioSignatures to Harmonize Hepatitis

Dr. Karim then created BioSignatures—patterns that would resonate with organs. This, coupled with bringing in BG3, could help bring harmony to organs. In a National Hepatitis Clinical Trial in Egypt that tested the major drugs for hepatitis, the people administering the trial allowed Dr. Karim to use BioSignatures to harmonize the liver. The study used certain liver enzymes to follow the course of the disease (increased enzyme levels occur when there is damage to the liver). The results from use of the BioSignatures were superior to those of all of the drugs tested.

There are many other studies that Dr. Karim carried out with amazing success (e.g., growing sweet potatoes in salt water from the Red Sea). The key is that bringing in harmony to the water showed amazing results.

There are wonderful courses available for learning BioGeometry. Check out the Vesica Institute (*https://vesica.org/*), or BioGeometry headquarters for a complete listing of BioGeometry courses (*https://www.biogeometry.ca/courses-events*).

Additional Tools

In addition to BioSignatures, there are other tools, usually having a geometric structure, which can be used to harmonize an environmental space and the people in that environment. There are now thousands of practitioners who work with BioGeometry for various purposes, including harmonizing homes, harmonizing the effects of electromagnetic fields, and harmonizing energy flows in organs for healing. Learning about the tools and science of BioGeometry through courses is the ideal way to understand the field. Tools include BioSignature pendants and rings, 90-degree L-pendant and stickers, Home Kit with Cubes, cell phone harmonizers, and other tools. There are various distributors, which can be found at *https://www.biogeometry.ca/official-retailers*. One such organization is *https://fmbr.org/*

Using BioGeometry Tools to Understand Our Role as Creators

Not only can we use BioGeometry tools to protect us and raise our level of harmony, but we also can achieve a better understanding of who we really are as creators. Through understanding the science of BioGeometry, we learn that we can affect the environment. We learn that we can bring in harmony to ourselves, to others, and to the environment. We also learn that we can send these harmonizing energies to distal locations to help others heal and to help heal the planet. We learn that location is not critical when we want to affect a person or an environment at another location. We start learning about our true potential.

Summary of Key Points in This Chapter

- The presence of Harmony is important in healing.
- The ability to work with subtle energies has taken place since antiquity, as evidenced in locating sacred sites for construction of temples, cathedrals, pyramids, etc.
- BioGeometry is a new science, developed by Dr. Ibrahim Karim, which brings the harmonizing and centering quality of BG3 into an environment.

- The One Harmonizing Subtle Energy Quality of BG3 can be detected by its resonance with three basic qualities: the higher harmonic of gold, the higher harmonic of ultraviolet, and "horizontal negative green."
- There are ways to increase BG3 by using shapes, geometric structures, angles, colors, designs, locations of objects, colors, sounds, and numbers (units, not numerals).
- You can use BG3 to affect your environment. Harmonizing an environment can result in positive, measurable outcomes, such as harmonizing the negative effects of electromagnetic fields (cell towers), allowing salt water to grow sweet potatoes, and normalizing clinical outcomes regarding diseases such as hepatitis.
- For the purpose of this book, bringing in harmony is a key element in healing and bringing in balance.

Notes

[1] Leon Chaumery and De Belizal developed key instruments for radiesthesia as well as the color scales used today to identify the subtle energies. The field of radiesthesia suffered a major setback when Chaumery was found mummified by his fellow scientist, de Belizal. The energy Chaumery was investigating had a strong detrimental and dehydrating effect and he did not know the magnitude of that effect. This is akin to Madame Curie dying from the effects of radiation from her discovery and work with radium. This was described in *Essai de Radiesthesie Vibratoire* (4th edition) by Leon Chaumery and A. de Belizal. 1976: Desforges, Paris; and *Physique Micro-Vibratoire et Forces Invisibles* by A. de Belizal and P.A. Morel. 1976: Desforges, Paris.

[2] While the French were developing their tools, primarily using various types of pendulums and the relationships of color with the subtle energies, the Germans developed other tools, primarily antennas. With these antennas, they identified different types of Earth Grids. These grids are a few feet or meters apart and are named for their discoverers. The Hartmann Grids run North-South and East-West; the Curry Grids run diagonal to the Hartmann lines. These lines are on the Earth as well as above the Earth. Benker Grids are characterized by their three-dimensional aspects. Where grid lines intersect and when they intersect with underground water, the BioGeometry energy quality of BG3, as measured by a BG3 pendulum, goes counterclockwise (detrimental). If a bed is located at such a site, health problems

can arise such as cancers. If you see trees that are quite gnarled, or you see a row of bushes and there's a space where bushes don't grow, these are indicative of such grid/underground water crossings. See descriptions in *BioGeometry: Back to a Future for Mankind,* by Ibrahim Karim.

CHAPTER 10

Healing — Harmony and the Self (I AM)

Everything that is of matter depends on polarity for its creation. This polarity naturally seeks equilibrium/ balance — like a seesaw, with God at the fulcrum of the center.

Now that you have been introduced in Chapter 9 to an understanding of harmony in relation to BioGeometry, it's time to explore how harmony applies to healing, and the connection between healing and I AM.

After studying and practicing healing for many years, I find that Joachim Wippich's simple yet profound teachings are at the heart of it. Joachim's principles of healing also have aspects found in BioGeometry, as well as in the crystal healing work of scientist Marcel Vogel (more on him later in this chapter). Aspects of the essence of Joachim's principles may also be reflected in other forms of healing as described later in this chapter as we discuss Reiki, spiritual healing, Quantum Touch, Pearl method, Bengston method, OMnium method, Dalian method, and other modalities. (Chapter 11 will go into Joachim's background, and the details of his teachings through affirmations to bring people to the truth of who they are and how to heal.)

There are three fundamental keys to healing, as taught by Joachim. Now that you have become familiar with the background of the fundamental points of I AM and harmony in Chapters 1–9, you can appreciate these three fundamental keys:

1. You *are* your thoughts and knowingness. You own your thoughts and create with your thoughts. Some of Joachim's affirmations state, "I own my thoughts" or "I am rethinking — rethink my thoughts within thoughts."
2. You can invite in harmony for the cells or the essential aspects of the situation (infections, trauma, disease, etc.), and have the cells or aspects recognize the disharmony that has been created. Once the disharmony is recognized, then harmony (healing) can occur.
3. You can bring the self to a place where you will remember that you are truly the Self, or I AM. At that point, your vibrational level moves to the I AM vibration frequency. The cells recognize the situation, and therefore revert to a state of harmony. Healing then occurs.

Joachim's Message on Harmony and Healing

Let's further discuss the relationship between harmony and healing, since bringing yourself into harmony is fundamental to healing.

The existence of polarity means that imbalances can and will occur. Everything that is of matter depends on polarity for its creation. This is because two polar aspects of spiraling light motion are compressed to form matter (based on Walter Russell's cosmology—refer to Chapter 4). This polarity naturally seeks equilibrium/balance. It is akin to a seesaw, with God at the fulcrum of the center. Our I AM centers at the fulcrum. When imbalance occurs, the whole system seeks to rebalance.

At the planetary level, rebalancing could be earthquakes to re-establish balance on the crust of the earth. On a human relationship level, rebalancing could be two divergent opinions needing to find a common ground to prevent conflict. At the national level, this same problem of conflicting opinions occurs between political parties, or between nations needing to settle a variety of conflicts.

Within the individual, because we have polarities within ourselves (e.g., we have our yin/yang aspects, masculine and feminine), we can have internal conflicts. For example, we can hold within us anger, fear, discordant memories, perceptions of injustice, physical trauma, childhood abuse, sexual abuse, karma from previous lifetimes, and so on.

When the disharmony manifests as an illness/disease/pain, then harmony/balance needs to be restored. The way Joachim teaches us is *to invite harmony with the disharmony*. By specifying the cells, the immune system, or any other problems that are in disharmony and needing to be harmonized, in essence he is seeking to restore the state of balance. This works because when the cells or organs that are in disharmony *realize they are behaving in a disharmonious way*, they will move back to harmony, and healing will occur.

Joachim often uses affirmations to bring in the harmony and to help people remember that they really are the I AM. In so doing, they self-heal, since harmony is achieved at the right I AM vibrational level.

Here is what Joachim says about harmony:

> By coming into harmony and love with disharmony, you disempower any non-beneficial energy. It no longer needs to be neutralized, released, transformed, or shooed away. I know that this process is complete when I have a steady, constant speed in the YES direction of my dowsing tool. If I am not getting the steady confirmation, I establish myself at a higher or more correct vibrational frequency and repeat my request to come into harmony with all disharmony.

Joachim on the I AM

A fundamental aspect of Joachim's teachings is the understanding of I AM. As expressed in the Introduction as well as Chapter 6, each of us is One with God. There is no separation. We are the thought creation of God throughout our evolution. We are immortal; there is no real death, just the death of our body — our material aspect.

A key factor influencing our healing is to remember and come to understand our true Divine nature and Oneness with God. As we come to that realization, our vibrational state is raised to the I AM level, where true healing can occur.

Joachim encourages people to affirm the "I AM" statement. He says:

> I invite people to come to the place of perfect light, divine harmony and love, [and then] their [pendulum] readings turn to a YES...

every time. Their soul is now in harmony, far beyond the physical level. They dowse (and heal) from the place of I AM. When I AM is said, it refers to the pure, loving essence of YOU. The divine individual [whom] God created to manifest your life on earth physically, spiritually and emotionally. As you refer to yourself in that way, you open up your heart and mind for divine inspiration. Realization of I AM brings the person to the divine vibrational level.

(The "Harmony and Raising the Vibrational Level to I AM" affirmation in Chapter 11 is an excellent one for achieving Harmony and the I AM vibrational state.)

In the next sections of this chapter, you will see that Walter Russell, Marcel Vogel, and BioGeometry have come to similar conclusions about the importance of harmony in the healing process.

Polarities Seek Harmony/Balance at the Center

To further understand the elements of harmony, let's return to Walter Russell's point that creation is made from polar elements, and that God is at the center — the point of balance. (Refer to Chapter 4 for more on Walter Russell's findings.)

The diagram below describes the male and female polar elements seeking balance.

The natural state is one of balance/harmony. However, you can see in the above diagram the possibility of *im*balances/*dis*harmony. Due to innate polarity and not remembering the Oneness of all, it is possible to move to a state of imbalance/disharmony. Disharmony results in conflicts and illness; thus, there is a need to *seek harmony with the disharmony* to achieve balance.

The *center* is the location of balance/harmony. (You can see this in the above diagram, at the fulcrum.) The greater the deviation from the center/balance, the greater the disharmony. In all situations, the solution is to move the situation towards the center, the point of balance. Key tools to achieve this harmony include: being non-judgmental; having compassion; having forgiveness; and love. This is applicable on all levels: to personal situations; to relations with others; and to relations with community, country, and with nations.

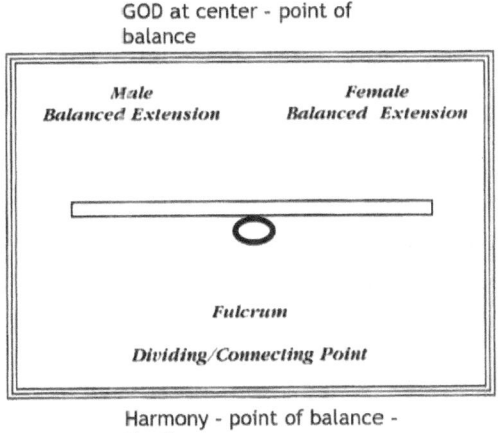

FIGURE 22. The male and female polar elements seeking balance

Marcel Vogel: Lessons in Healing

Marcel Vogel was an enlightened scientist working at IBM. He did experiments with plants, following the work of Cleve Backster, and found that communications with plants were linked to the experimenter's breath and thought, regardless of distance. The plants' responsiveness to thought was the same whether the person was eight inches away, eight feet away, or a thousand miles away. He found that plants responded more to the *thought* of being cut, burned, or torn than to the actual act.

This work eventually led him to study quartz crystals. From a vision that he received, he was led to create a multi-faceted crystal—now known as the "Vogel-cut®" crystal—in the shape of the Tree of Life. He learned that this crystal could store, amplify, and transmit coherent subtle energies. This led to research on the therapeutic application of quartz crystals.

Vogel's healing procedure consisted of the following steps:

1. Clearing the crystal with an exhalation of breath and the intent to clear the crystal.
2. Charging the crystal with loving intent (harmony).
3. Using the crystal, linking with the energy system of the subject (the person needing healing) at the thymus gland, just below the breastbone. (The thymus is an essential component of our immune system.)
4. Instructing the subject to go to the location of disharmonious energy in the body.
5. Having the healer and the subject breathe together to achieve resonance of energies.
6. Having both the healer and subject explosively breathe out.
7. The subject thus expels disharmonious energy and makes room for harmonious energy from the crystal.
8. The subject thus heals himself or herself by bringing in the harmonious energy to replace the disharmonious energy.

One thing we can learn from Vogel's healing technique is that *the person needing healing* (the subject) brings in harmony (harmonious energy) to displace disharmony—that is, that it's being done by the person needing healing and not by the person holding the crystal (the healer). The healer is simply making the harmonious energy available to the person needing the healing.

Inviting Harmony into What Needs Healing

This concept is like Joachim's procedure when he asks the person needing healing to invite in harmony to the part of the body that needs healing.

Healing Arises from Positive, Harmonizing Loving Energies

The various modalities of energy healing—such as Reiki, Jane Katra's spiritual healing, Richard Gordon's Quantum Touch, Eric Pearl's connection, Bill Bengston's cycling, the OMnium method, the Dalian method of healing into consciousness, and others—have some commonalities. For one thing, most healers do not claim to understand exactly *how* they are able to heal. Most healers give positive, loving energies, with the intent for healing to occur.

Note that this chapter is not intended to cover *all* forms of alternative healing. Almost all of them will have loving intentions of healing, but may also have other modalities involved. Some methods may involve transmitting BG3 qualities, elevating the vibrational frequencies of the individual, and bringing in harmony and love. They may do this by use of subtle energies (e.g., pranic healing techniques, Reiki, and other methods); scalar energies from instruments; color and sound therapies using elements of vibrational energies to impact a health problem; body talk to communicate with the body as to the nature of the problem; Emotional Freedom Technique (EFT), which taps on acupuncture points to communicate with a problem and bring it into consciousness; meditations and guided communications to bring a problem to the surface of consciousness to resolve it, as in the Dalian Method; essential oils; stones/minerals/gems; and many other methods not listed here. However, I find that the Harmony Affirmations and bringing a person to the I AM vibrational level, as taught by Joachim Wippich, are at the heart of healing, harmony/balance, and health.

As humans, we naturally give off the harmonizing, centering energy of BG3 (*see* Chapter 9) when we hold the intention of love/harmony. Humans can store and release this energy in a quartz (Vogel) crystal. The commonality among all these healing modalities is the bringing in of harmonizing, loving energies, and, in the process, raising the level of vibration.

Harmony, BioGeometry, and Healing

In Chapter 9, we discussed some of the elements of BioGeometry in relation to Harmony—such as resonance with BG3, which results in harmonization. As mentioned, harmonization is often a prerequisite for healing.

Harmonization can be directed to the environment or to a specific location (such as an organ). BioGeometry tools can be used to help balance the environment or an organ (e.g., with BioSignatures, to be in resonance with the organ).

The Energies of Disease

BioGeometry is based on the view that disease states have specific detrimental energy qualities, which can be measured. These negative energy qualities are present in the following conditions:[1]

- Lies
- Negative states of thought and emotion (as well as suppression of natural healthy thought and feeling)
- Active disease states
- Electro-magnetic and other toxic radiations
- Toxic components of Earth Energy Grids
- Detrimental spiritual (non-physical) forces

Disease can be reinforced and intensified by resonance with the above phenomena.

Disease is a combination of the imbalance itself *and* the body's corrective reaction. Whenever there is a disease problem, the body attempts to correct the imbalance. For example, having a fever and runny nose is the body's attempt to rid itself of the virus. Likewise, inflammation is the body's attempt to bring in the macrophages and cytokines needed to mount an attack on the invading virus or bacteria.

Most diseases are the result of inflammation fighting a problem, as interpreted by the body. Unfortunately, often the inflammatory process itself is the cause of the disease or problem (e.g., arthritis and autoimmune diseases are caused by the body fighting itself).

At the physical, emotional, and mental levels, there can be imbalances that result in disease. However, at the Divine level, balance/harmony is always present.

Environmental Aspects of Disease

Diseases may also have environmental aspects. We are all part of larger collective levels than our own surroundings, alone. And it's not only environmental aspects on a *physiological* level (e.g., the effects on our bodies of the air we breathe); this also happens on a *mental* level. The higher level of depression due to people being separated from one another during the COVID pandemic could be an example. Collective beliefs about a disease can result in the physical manifestation of those beliefs.

The belief that a disease is deadly may mean that the person who has the disease will have an expectation of dying. Joe Dispenza, the author of *You are the Placebo*, has repeatedly demonstrated that giving such persons a placebo and telling them that the new medical drug will make them healthy often results in healing. He describes miraculous cures for cancer and many other diseases by means of the placebo effect. Joachim and other healers often teach us not to give a label to a disease, since the label helps to solidify the disease as a real thought-form with a defined life based on collective beliefs. That is, every disease has a *collective influence* on the individual who experiences the disease. For example, people who are told they will die of cancer in three months will often die in three months; if they are told the cancer is in remission, they may live a long life.

Spiritual Aspects of Disease

Another view of disease is from a spiritual perspective. We may have reincarnated in this lifetime to learn some lessons. The disease is a challenge that will cause us to focus and overcome both the challenge and the disease. To overcome the condition of having negative resonance with others, we may need to learn the value of unconditional blessing, forgiveness, and gratitude.

If we get mad at people who harm us, we can come to realize that—from a higher perspective—they are simply the messenger from the Divine who is here to create situations to help us learn. At a higher level, it is like taking an exam to test our ability to achieve the center/harmony. Our task is to learn to always connect the exam (what we are to learn) and the center together. Learning to be non-judgmental, loving, compassionate, and forgiving helps bring us to the center.

Fear as a Basis of Disease

From another perspective, *fear* is a factor in sickness. Fear has many forms. It can be fear of being sick. It can be fear of not getting what we desire, or of losing what we have. As mentioned earlier, negative thoughts—including fear, lies, being judgmental, blaming, and being unable to forgive—result in lower vibrational levels. Lower vibrational levels, in turn, result in a lowering of our immune system, making us more susceptible to infections and other health problems.

Moving into harmony and the I AM vibrational level—such as through love, gratitude, compassion, and forgiveness—moves a person out of the fear and negative-thought level.

Our thoughts affect not only ourselves but also those whom we think about. Positive, loving thoughts rather than judgmental, blaming thoughts will affect our health and the health of others positively or negatively. Seeing the Divine in others and in all things is what we should strive to do. The Divine is in all things.

Fighting a Disease

When you fight a disease by attacking it, the consciousness of the disease is aware of it and will fight back. We enhance the disease by giving it a name and talking about it. The disease is like an entity, but that entity is part of us. The disease may be energetically linked with us. The disease may also have a spiritual aspect, to teach us something we need to learn. From the BioGeometry perspective, in healing we bring in the centering/harmonizing quality of BG3 and allow what needs to happen to occur.

In Joachim Wippich's teaching, one invites the disease problem to come into harmony with its own disharmony. By doing this, the disease realizes that it is causing disharmony for the person and often will disengage from causing disharmony. Joachim's strategy is not to attack, but to *invite in harmony*.

Healing Disease with BioGeometry

In BioGeometry, we work with bringing in the centering/harmony resonant quality of BG3 to the environment. An organ in a person can also be considered as an *inner* environment. BioGeometry does not actively "treat" any illness; however, by bringing in harmony/centering, a disease or illness may be healed. Healing is connected to a higher wisdom, which determines the outcome once the person has been connected to the center. Sometimes healing may occur for one person and not another person.

Real healing has to do with transforming the person's life, not with symptom relief. BioGeometry is not a form of medicine. It is simply an environmental support. Environmental support is very important in itself; it is a preventive medicine and can stop other potential problems, even if a given illness presents itself.

BioGeometry has many tools for bringing in the centering/harmonizing subtle-energy quality of BG3. For example, for bringing BG3 into the home, there is the Home Kit with Cubes, which have symbols or numbers to create BG3. There are BioSignature pendants or rings, which can resonate with the organs of the individual to bring in BG3. BG3 can even be brought in for a person or situation at a distance. If a person is working remotely and bringing BG3 to another individual, there are "Emitter Sheets" with BioGeometry symbols to enhance the sending out of BG3. In that case, we would use a "witness" of a person on the Emitter Sheet so that healing can occur non-locally. A "witness" can be a photograph of a person or some cells from a person on a small piece of paper. The use of a "witness" is very common in radiesthesia, BioGeometry, healing with dowsing, and almost all forms of alternative healing from a distance. In healing and connecting with others, distance is immaterial.

Summary of Key Points in This Chapter

In this chapter, we have looked at healing from a number of viewpoints:
- Bringing in Harmony/Balance/Centering and loving intention are primary components of healing.
- Being at the I AM vibrational level is the other key component of healing.
- Many other healing modalities likely use elements of the above points, bringing in harmony by the loving intention to heal, which brings in centering and BG3. Energetic connection to persons being healed also likely helps to elevate a person's vibrational energy level.

- Most healers typically do not know how or when healing might occur, when their methods are used. BioGeometry explains this phenomenon by stating that BG3 harmonizes/centers the environment for healing to occur, but the healing occurs based on a higher wisdom.
- Marcel Vogel echoes these points — his Vogel crystals supply the required healing energies (loving intention), but the healing is done by the person being healed.
- Walter Russell similarly describes the centering concept as the balance needed with the opposing male/female lights, which are the basis of creation.
- BioGeometry analyzes: the negative conditions that lower BG3; how BG3 harmonizes/centers the environment; the spiritual aspects of a disease as a teaching tool; how fear is a factor in disease; and how harmonizing a disease may be a better alternative than fighting it.

Notes

[1] From "Notes on the Disease Forming Process," by Dr. Ibrahim Karim, in the BioGeometry Course.

CHAPTER 11

Joachim Wippich — Teacher of Light

On Joachim's background, his principles for creating harmony and raising your level of vibration, his "pearls of wisdom," and points for you to consider when stating affirmations.

A primary purpose of this book is to present the valuable teachings of Joachim Wippich. The first half of the book has set forth the essential elements of Joachim's teachings concerning harmony, healing, and the meaning of I AM, all of which are key to understanding our true origins.

In this chapter, you will find out about Joachim's background, his principles for creating harmony, raising your level of vibration, his "pearls of wisdom," and points to consider when stating affirmations. A collection of some of Joachim's Affirmations also appears in this chapter.

Joachim's Background

Joachim Wippich was born in Germany. Gifted with the ability to pick up new knowledge and skills easily, he has worked in many different capacities. Yet no matter what profession he entered into, he brought in intuition and extraordinary skills. He has been a baker, a farmer, a metal worker/machinist, a truck driver, and a glass and optics fabricator. In Silicon Valley, he worked for five startups and five large corporations.

As a young boy growing up in Germany, he worked as a baker. He later got a job on a farm. In addition to being a hard worker, he had an unusual ability to communicate with animals, especially horses. He understood what they wanted.

Joachim served as an apprentice in the metal-working/machinist industry. He understands machines and knows how to make them work. In Silicon Valley, Joachim worked for a number of large and small companies. He was always invaluable, since he was often the experienced person who could figure out how to solve difficult problems.

For example, when a company was not able to figure how to polish a mirror to the degree needed for a telescope to be launched in space, Joachim would instinctively know the mechanism to accomplish the task. He often encountered similar issues when corporations wanted to make precision optical products, and no one in the company could solve the problems to accomplish the goal. Joachim would be called in on the case and would fix the issue.

Joachim also started his own glass-and-optics company, which he eventually sold when he started dowsing.

Joachim's Entry into Dowsing

As with Joachim's other careers, when he got into the area of dowsing and healing, his insights went to the heart of the nature of both. He realized that disharmony (or imbalance) was at the heart of many problems, as disharmony is innate to the human condition. He realized that we are all Divine Beings with a connection to God, and thus have the ability to invite in harmony to achieve a balance with the disharmony.

Joachim was introduced to dowsing 40 years ago by his dowsing mentors, Bob Mahany and Pete Warburton, both members of the San Jose Dowsers. Both Mahany and Warburton were wonderful dowsers. Pete was a marvelous healer. It was he who started the tradition of meeting at a coffee shop on Saturdays to help anyone desiring healing.

Joachim's particular focus in dowsing is to assist others with self-healing. He developed his own unique system for healing, incorporating fine-tuned harmony/disharmony affirmations along with his dowsing to help people understand the nature of harmony/disharmony and remember who they truly are — I AM — and thus reach the necessary vibrational levels for healing.

Since, among Joachim's many careers, he was once a precision machinist, he used his skill to make a unique precision L-rod for dowsing, which he personally designed and produced. Joachim is also an intuitive who sees and knows the nature of people's problems, and is thus exceptional at giving them the right affirmations for healing.

Helping People Heal Themselves

Every Saturday at noon, Joachim shows up at a coffee shop in Cupertino, CA. Before long, there are about 10-20 people congregating around him. He often stays for a good portion of the afternoon, helping them.

The people are there for a wide variety of reasons. Many are there to be healed of a physical ailment, an emotional problem, or an illness of a friend. Others are there for the wisdom he imparts. And still others are there to be reminded of who they truly are, and thus bring up their vibrations to the I AM level. When Joachim was asked why he comes out to do this on a weekly basis, he said, "My purpose is to help people come into the light."

Healing Tools: The L-Rod

At these Saturday gatherings, Joachim will bring out his special dowsing rod, the L-rod. It has ball bearings, which allow it to be exquisitely easy to rotate. One of his purposes in using the dowsing rod is to allow him to know the vibrational level of the person coming to get advice or healing. When a person is truly at the I AM level, the dowsing rod will whirl rapidly. Healing is difficult if the person is at a low vibrational level, and the L-rod will quickly reveal this.

Joachim is sensitive enough that, even without the dowsing rod, he knows the nature of the problem and the person's vibrational level. But he is not there to heal others; he's there to teach the people to heal themselves. In fact, Joachim says that *he* is not doing the healing, they are.

Healing Tools: Affirmations

To facilitate this self-healing, Joachim will give the people affirmations to repeat in order to remind them of who they really are. He may gently help them along to reach that higher I AM vibrational level, but he continuously teaches them to reach that higher level themselves.

Healing Tools: Inviting the Cells to Come into Harmony with the Disharmony

Another key lesson he teaches is that *everyone can communicate with their whole being* — with all the cells and systems/organs in their body. Diseases/ailments occur when there is disharmony in the body/emotions. Joachim teaches how to invite the cells or immune system to come into harmony. All cells and bacteria/viruses have their own intelligence. The discordant cells may not know that they are in disharmony with the rest of the body, and so need to have communications from the person, inviting them into harmony.

Our cells and our entire being are built to be in harmony or balance. But everything that is of matter can become unbalanced and be in a state of disharmony. For healing to occur, all that is necessary is to invite the cells to come into harmony with the disharmony. The cells, having innate consciousness/intelligence, will understand that they need to come into harmony/balance with the disharmony/imbalance. When that occurs, healing occurs.

Remembering Our Divine Nature (I AM)

In the Saturday sessions at the coffee house, there is often a need for people to be reminded of their divine lineage — that they are truly I AM. We are brought up and educated to give power to others to be the authority figures over our lives — whether it be parents, doctors, teachers, priests, the government, etc. Thus, we act as if others have the responsibility for our lives, and we turn everything over to them.

But ultimately, we have to realize that each one of us is Divine, and that each person is amazing. Joachim fully understands this point, so one of his important affirmations is to say:

"I am amazingly delightful."

He finds that many people cannot make that statement. But Joachim is persistent and will coach people until they *can* make that statement. It is hard for people to come to the realization that they are each I AM, as well as to realize how amazingly delightful they are — and to be able to make that statement.

Joachim teaches that we create from our thoughts. Our thoughts create our reality. We are responsible for our thoughts. Thus, Joachim teaches us to "rethink" our thoughts.

The lessons Joachim teaches on Saturdays are life-changing for those in attendance. It may take many Saturdays of learning for a person to come to the same level of understanding that Joachim has. Thus, his Saturdays are always full of people eager for healing and learning.

On the second Saturday of the month, Joachim forgoes his coffee house gathering and teaches dowsing, especially dowsing for healing, at the meeting room of the San Jose Dowsers, a Chapter of the American Society of Dowsers. We typically come for a lecture from an invited speaker. Before and after the lecture, Joachim will meet with individuals who want to receive advice/healing from him.

As people start to learn Affirmations from Joachim at the weekly coffee shop gathering, they see that Joachim offers many pearls of wisdom on a variety of points and conditions. The next section provides a collection of these pearls. Some I may have stated previously, but they are put here all in one place to offer a *collection* of these pearls.

Pearls of Wisdom from Joachim Wippich

Free Will: Invite Rather Than Command

There is a world of difference between "ask" and "invite." All of life has free will. When you "ask" that something be done, in essence it is a command. "Please do" is also a command. However, when you "invite," you are leaving free will to make the decision. Since life naturally desires harmony/balance, life invariably will listen and the invitation will be heeded.

Thus it is better to, as Joachim puts it, "invite cells, which have an activity of pain, to come into harmony with their disharmony." The cells will then realize that there is disharmony and automatically come into harmony; healing then occurs. The same approach can be used with an infection. A bacteria can be invited to come into harmony with its disharmony.

On Pain and Disease

Giving a label to a dysfunction helps to *solidify* the dysfunction. The dysfunction then becomes a part of the body, part of you. It will then have its own life. It becomes "my diabetes" or "my migraine," or whatever the condition might be.

Rather than give it a name, refer to it as an *activity*, or use another word to describe the condition. Do not empower the condition. A person can say "my cancer" and the doctor will say, "With your cancer, you can expect to live 6 months." The cancer will then have its life, and your life is now limited.

Vibrational Level

It is good to get into the habit of checking your vibrational level. You might feel lethargic, or a desired healing does not seem to be occurring. The problem might be that you are not entirely present in your body.

You should then state the affirmation to bring you back to the I AM, and simultaneously dowse to check your vibrational level. The spin of your L-rod or pendulum will let you know when you are back to the I AM level. We will describe these affirmations later in this chapter. (It was also described in Chapter 8, on dowsing.)

Questions versus Statements Properly Worded

Joachim has made an important observation, one that he now uses in his affirmations: *Questions sometimes get questionable answers.* A properly worded statement of fact, on the other hand, said with understanding and connection to that statement, results in a change in the person. For example, saying, "I thank you so much" is a limiting statement, but saying, "I thank you so *very* much" is expansive and not limiting. A similar analogy can be made between "I love you so much" as compared to "I love you so *very* much."

Another powerful statement Joachim makes is to say:

"I am in harmony with my disharmony."

This is a statement that you are truly in harmony. It recognizes that disharmony can be there, but you are now in *balance* with the disharmony. Joachim has many carefully worded affirmations.

Not Letting the Mind Wander

Sometimes people may let the mind wander and when they come back, there may be a bit of fatigue and disorientation. It is because they have left the body and have not paid attention to it. Joachim's precaution is not to allow the mind to wander off for too long. His instructions are:

"Mind, please go to the universal mind and bring back to me what I need to know for my next step. Please do not stay away for more than a minute every hour."

Some people may respond, "Why only one minute?"

Joachim then stretches this to three minutes. "You don't want to go away for more than three minutes," he explains, "because you might forget to come back. Then what happens is that you really get drained, and you cannot even think about why you were getting drained. So I would just go for one minute. Once you do this, then you get your energy back."

Allowing Creativity and Knowingness to Enter

After bringing your vibration to the I AM level (which you can check with your L-rod or pendulum), say:

"I open my door of knowingness and am inviting greater thoughts to come through in a creative form."

Then things appear in your mind—maybe not this instant, but five minutes from now, or sometime today, or whenever. Knowing that this will come about really gives you peace.

Then stillness sets in. Even if there's noise around you, there is stillness around you. It is just like a meditation. In the beginning, you probably won't feel this right away, but maybe you will. You will evolve by doing this and you can fulfill your evolutionary divine thought creation.

An alternative statement that Joachim sometimes uses is:

> "Mind, go to the universal mind and bring back to me what I need to know for my next evolutionary step."

The Importance of Your Full Birth Name and of Stating It

Typically, at the end of many of Joachim's affirmations, to bring the vibration to the I AM level, the person is instructed to state:

> "I AM self-correcting my evolutionary thoughts creations 100% 24/7 I AM [Full Birth Name] I AM."

There is power in your Full Birth Name. You came into this incarnation to live your life for its various purposes, and were gifted with your Full Birth Name as your identity. Stating that identity brings you into alignment with your I AM. You feel that impact as you state your full name, followed by "I AM."

The "Rethink" Concept, Linked with I AM

When a person does not realize something at the deepest level, having that person rethink the thought often allows her or him to come to a deep understanding of the concept. The concept of your true identity is such a concept. Thus, Joachim will ask the person to state:

> "I AM rethinking — rethink I AM"

or:

> "I AM inviting Thoughts to rethink with me."

In the above statements, Joachim uses the concept of "rethinking — rethink." This set of words energetically produces a pause, and invites the person to re-evaluate the words "I AM." The objective of the pause is to allow the person to come to the realization of the true meaning of I AM. When the person realizes who he or she really is (I AM), the vibration level goes up, as confirmed by the dowsing rod or rotating pendulum.

The Flow of the Thought in Affirmations and Punctuation

With affirmations, Joachim often views punctuation marks as interfering with the flow of the thought. Thus, you will see many places where an English major or grammatical expert will say that the statement needs a period or a comma. However, Joachim will not put in the punctuation, since it breaks up the sequence of words that form the flow of the thought. What Joachim has often found is that the words without the punctuation are energetically more powerful than if they had punctuation.

The 3-6-9 Concept

In the final chapter of this book, you will learn the wonder of the 3-6-9 concept.

3-6-9 is embedded in all the key creation symbols. Nikola Tesla—the inventor, engineer, and physicist who invented Alternating Current (AC) generation and transmission technology—used 3-6-9 to help bring in the creative energies in many of his amazing inventions. The numbers have significance in terms of creation, enlightenment, and who we are. In the chapter on 3-6-9, you will read that, at our core, we have the energies of 3-6-9.

Joachim teaches that when affirmations are repeated three times, six times, and nine times, they are significantly augmented with the energy of the Divine. When a person is "stuck" in bringing in understanding of an important concept to enable healing to occur, Joachim will ask that person to repeat the affirmation (or a portion of the affirmation) three times...pause...then six times...pause...then nine times. This sequence invariably allows the person to break through the blocks of understanding so that healing can occur.

In some of the affirmations in this book, the affirmation or a portion of the affirmation will have after it the words "3x, 6x and 9x." This means you should repeat the affirmation or portions of it 3 times, then 6 times, and then 9 times. It is a shorthand way to give the instruction that you should repeat the affirmation or portion of it 3 times, then 6 times, and again 9 times. At other times the affirmation may be repeated 3 times, 6 times, and 9 times so that you don't have to keep count as to how many times you have repeated it. Affirmations can be read out loud, or silently, or done mentally as your thoughts.

On the Misuse of the Word "So"

The right brain interprets words literally. When you use the word "so" by itself, it means a limited amount. Thus, when you say, "I love you so much" or "I thank you so much," it means that you are offering a limited amount of love or thanks. When Joachim tests for your level of vibration, the use of "so" in this context results in a reduction in your vibrational energy.

On the other hand, your vibrational energy goes up when you say, "I love you so *very* much," or "I thank you so *very* much." The qualifier of "very" extends rather than limits.

Use Coming into Balance/Harmony Rather Than Clearing

Dowsers often "clear" themselves before dowsing to increase their accuracy. Joachim teaches that one does not "clear." Nothing is "wiped out." Instead, one brings in balance or harmony.

The beginning of Joachim's Harmony Dowsing affirmation is an excellent way to achieve balance. In that affirmation, women invite the left brain and right brain to join together with the heart. Then they invite the right brain and left brain to join together with the heart. Men would do the same, but reverse the order, starting with the right brain and ending with the left brain.

When making these statements, it helps to spread your arms out and bring them together as you unite the left brain, right brain, and heart to come together. This affirmation section will be described in detail in the Harmony Dowsing affirmation.

On Being Amazingly Delightful (ancillary: "I Love Myself" or "I Am Excellent")

Since many persons have given over their power to others throughout their lives (teachers, bosses, governments, religious leaders, etc.), their self-esteem is low. They do not understand their Divine lineage—that they are I AM and a thought creation of God. As such, they have a hard time saying that they are "amazingly delightful" or "I love myself" or "I am excellent."

Thus, Joachim teaches people to say, "I am amazingly delightful" or "I love myself" or "I am loving myself" (this means a continuous state of loving oneself). When the thought of "amazingly delightful" or "love myself" registers with the individual, the vibrational frequency automatically goes up, as seen by dowsing.

Realizing That You Are Your Thoughts

Two related phrases Joachim teaches are:

"I am my thoughts" and "I am rethinking — rethink my thoughts."

One can even repeat the statement by saying:

"I am rethinking — rethink my thoughts within thoughts"

and by repeating the "within thoughts" 3 times, 6 times, and 9 times. Since you *are* your thoughts and are creating with your thoughts, repeating the "within thoughts" 3 times, 6 times, and 9 times brings you back to your original thought creation and vibrational level, and empowers you to be your Divine I AM. This repetition is written below for better understanding:

3x: "I am rethinking — rethink my thoughts within thoughts within thoughts"

6x: "I am rethinking — rethink my thoughts within thoughts within thoughts within thoughts within thoughts within thoughts"

9x: "I am rethinking — rethink my thoughts within thoughts within thoughts within thoughts within thoughts within thoughts within thoughts within thoughts within thoughts"

The next step is to say:

"I AM in Harmony with my thoughts I AM"

and:

"I AM owning my thoughts I AM."

Thus, you take full responsibility and ownership for your thoughts.

The Effects of Thoughts on Healing

Sometimes healings can be hindered by one's thoughts. These can be thoughts about commonly accepted outcomes of a disease (e.g., cancer, etc.), or thoughts of blame as the cause for a problem, or unresolved disagreements that have become chronic. Taking ownership of those thoughts is a first step. Thus Joachim recommends:

"I AM responsible for my healing thoughts."

Determining If a Class, Book, or Course Is Good for You

In Joachim's group teachings, people would ask him many questions, such as how to select the most appropriate workshops, training, classes, books, etc. He then would state:

"I am inviting you to dowse the following:

'What percentage of True Harmony or Divine Harmony vibration frequency will this workshop/presentation or book create/generate for me? What percentage will *my* True Harmony or Divine Harmony vibration frequency be affected by attending this workshop/class or reading this book?'"

On Communicating with the Body

Each cell has consciousness and tries to please you. So don't say, "I have an illness"; instead, say, "I was diagnosed with an illness." There can be misunderstandings or misinterpretations in communications with cells in your body. For example, when you say, "I am in harmony with my pain," your body might interpret that to mean there is no pain or "I am okay with having the pain."

By stating, "I own the pain," you acknowledge it. It is good to find out who created it, and for what purpose. You can dowse for an answer. The body/interference needs your help, and you are not listening. You can gift with your harmony affirmation the parts of your body that experience pain by inviting those parts with pain to accept the harmony affirmation, and inviting the cells to come into harmony with the disharmony (i.e., come into balance). Invite them to rethink with you, and they change.

Your body/subconscious/right brain listens to the exact words you are saying. When you say, "Thank you so much," you have put a limitation on the amount of thankfulness. Instead say, "Thank you *very* much," or "Thank you so *very* much."

On Stress

Do not try to harmonize stress. "I AM in harmony with stress" does not relate to the problem. Stress is not the event, it is your *reaction*. What you want to harmonize is the "thought" of stress. So instead, state: "I invite the thought of stress to come into harmony with its own disharmony."

On Interfering Thoughts

Sometimes a person is at a lower vibrational state because of "interfering thoughts." Such thoughts can also be thought of as "hijacking thoughts." They cause the mind to be away from the I AM level. These may be thoughts that are reverberating in the mind about elections, politics, arguments that occurred in the past, etc. Whatever the cause, the net result is that the person is not "present," due to the interfering thoughts.

Joachim recommends stating:

> "I invite interfering thoughts [or hijacking thoughts] to come to their correct vibrational frequency to fulfill their own destiny."

This allows the thoughts to come to their conclusion and allows you to return to your I AM frequency.

On the Evolutionary Path and Joachim's Path

Joachim says this:

> "My definition for the evolutionary path is the following: I am energy and light. I came to this world to experience physicality and to try to help people to come into the light to fulfill their evolutionary thought creation. When I repeat 'I AM my evolutionary divine thought creation,' the pendulum or L-rod starts speeding up.
>
> "As your energy comes into your body, your spine straightens up. And if you want, use your pendulum to measure your reaction.

Everybody probably has a different idea as to their evolutionary path, but this is what I can share with you: I believe that my evolutionary path is to establish who I am, what I am, and what I do on this planet Earth in this physical body.

"If I come into harmony with my own disharmony, I come into harmony with everybody who wants to have harmony in their life. To harmonize my evolutionary path, the way I see it, I am inviting myself to come into harmony with my own disharmony throughout my evolutionary divine thought creation 100%.

"Use your pendulum or L-rod, and your subconscious mind knows the percentage. Come and be in harmony with your own disharmony 100%: 24/7 'I AM.' Please say it as if you really mean it. Just don't fly over this. This is very meaningful to you. Then say 'I AM' with your full birth name."

Being Yourself

Joachim has said:

"I'm just human. I have weaknesses. I make mistakes and I experience sadness. But I learn from all these things to make me a better person. Live your life the way that you want to live it. Don't let other people live it for you. Be bold enough to use your voice, brave enough to listen to your heart, and strong enough to live the life you've always imagined. Be true to yourself. You are the only person that matters.

"We were born to be true, not to be perfect. Why try to change who you are to make someone love you, when the right person will love you for who you really are? I am not in this world to live up to your expectations, and you are not in this world to live up to mine. Never apologize for showing your feelings. Never regret being who you truly are. For those who matter will love you no matter what!!!!!"

On Breath and Saying I AM

The vibrational energy of saying I AM is enhanced when "I" is stated with the inhalation of breath and "AM" is stated with the exhalation of breath. In meditation, to link to your essence, a lot of attention is paid to the breath. In Kriya Yoga, during meditation one is taught to say "Hong Sau" with breath, which translates to "I am He"; the essence of this translation is "I AM." In Walter Russell's terminology, inhalation is the spiraling creation cycle and the exhalation is the spiraling cycle of the breakdown of matter. Thus, stating "I" with the inhalation of breath (the creation portion of the cycle) and "AM" with the exhalation of breath (the breakdown portion of the cycle) represents the entire cycle and thus enhances the vibrational energy.

Some Affirmations by Joachim Wippich

Below are some useful affirmations by Joachim. The Table of Affirmations will help you find the affirmation you may be seeking.

Table of Affirmations

- Harmonic Dowsing
- Harmony for Mother Earth
- Affirmation for Healing Earth
- Harmony for the Physical Body
- An Alternative Harmony Affirmation for the Physical Body
- Harmony for the Immune System
- Knowledge within Cellular Thoughts
- Self-Correct When Not Feeling Well
- Memory or Immune System
- Harmonizing My Memory
- A Healing Affirmation
- For Harmonizing Breath and Regeneration
- Rethink
- Affirmation to Increase Your Vibrational Level (Useful for Dowsers)
- Alternative Harmony and Raising Vibrational Level to the I AM
- Knowledge
- Spiritual Evolution 1 and 2
- Getting a Good Night's Sleep

Harmonic Dowsing

[Reproduced from Joachim Wippich's brochure, *Harmonic Dowsing*]

I [Joachim] have found that there are three distinct preparations I use to ready myself and my students for dowsing:

1. **Invite both sides of your brain to join together with your heart.**

To enhance the power of the above words, it is helpful that you spread out your hands to the sides and bring them together so the palms meet while you invite the two halves of the brain and heart to come together. In addition, Step 1 can be used at any time, under any circumstance, to bring in balance and harmony. One does not need to be dowsing to bring in harmony with our brain and with our heart.

   a. For Women: "I invite my left brain and my right brain to join together with my heart. I invite my right brain and my left brain to join together with my heart I AM"

   b. For Men: "I invite my right brain and my left brain to join together with my heart. I invite my left brain and my right brain to join together with my heart I AM"

I often repeat the phrase, "I am aware that all components of my divine being are active, present and functioning at 100%." This process of bringing your entire physical and spiritual being into harmony establishes the energetic connection required for accurate dowsing results. Checking to see if the connection is complete brings us to the next phase.

2. **Test with your dowsing implement (pendulum, rods, bobber, or physical form of dowsing) to verify that the joining of both sides of your brain with your heart is complete.** You will know you are ready to move to the next step when there is a strong and steady "yes," or positive signal with your dowsing tool.

3. **Whether you are dowsing for yourself or others, prepare yourself to be safe and receptive to the energetic messages.** Effective dowsing answers the following questions:

a. WHO: I AM — followed by anyone else involved.
b. WHAT: Invite to be in 100% divine harmony with disharmony.
c. WHEN: Usually now, but you may go beyond this timing.
d. WHERE: This universe, this earth, this home, this place...
e. WHY: The particular reason to dowse at this time.
f. HOW: By bringing I AM, or the target into 100% harmony.

Often people enter the dowsing experience and ask to go to "Source Energy." My method ensures that the source the dowser accesses is in complete alignment with pure love, light, harmony and benevolence on all levels, 100%.

I believe in God, our loving, divine, supreme creator. He created us in His likeness to experience mortality with all of its joys and challenges. God did not leave us alone. We have been created for a purpose. We have the Spirit, or Light of Christ, to help guide us in our benevolent works. He gave us free will to choose for ourselves, His perfect plan allows for us to reject Him as our Divine Creator and live in circumstances other than love and harmony.

I invite you to ponder the fact that His design of pure love and harmony is available to each of us and we have a responsibility to make the world a better place through accessing His divine assistance. Dowsing is a powerful means to do this.

I respect that you may have another philosophy; use whatever works for you. However, I can say that as people challenge me, asking their source if my method is true, often their answer is "no." When I invite them to come to the place of perfect light, divine harmony and love, their readings turn to a "yes"...every time. Their soul is now in harmony, far beyond the physical level. They dowse from the place of I AM.

When "I AM" is said, it refers to the pure, loving essence of YOU. The divine individual God created to manifest your life on earth physically, spiritually and emotionally. As you refer to yourself in that way, you open up your heart and mind for divine inspiration.

I AM means accepting myself. "I" alone does not indicate continuity, which is also the reason for putting "I AM" at the end of a phrase.

Harmony

This is a phrase that I often use to bring my vibrational level to the frequency of pure love and well-being, visualized by white light surrounding me and those for whom I am dowsing.

By coming into harmony with disharmony, you disempower any non-beneficial energy. It no longer needs to be neutralized, released, transformed or shooed away. I know that this process is complete when I have a steady, constant speed in the "yes" direction of my dowsing tool. If I am not getting the steady confirmation, I establish myself at a higher or more correct vibrational frequency and repeat my request to come into harmony with disharmony.

Dowsing works whether or not you are in harmony with the highest and best vibrational frequency; however, the results are not the same if information is coming from another source. It is a fact that energy is impressed upon matter. I seek to teach people to reach for the purest, most loving and transformative energy in all of creation. This knowledge is my gift to you to assist you in blessing the lives and space of the people around you.

It is my continuous divine intention that I AM 100% resonant with all love and harmony within this world and universe. This vibrational frequency guides my entire reference point and fills me with emotional generosity.

If not, "Re-Think" until reaching 100% I AM.

With all of my love, generosity, harmony and gratitude,

Joachim

Harmony for Mother Earth

"I AM inviting every thought within every cell to please give yourself the permission and come to the correct vibration frequency of your first thought creation."

"I AM inviting you to place yourself equally spaced around the planet and project Divine Love, Divine Harmony, Divine Gratitude, Divine Forgiveness, Divine Light, Divine Life, Divine Happiness, Divine Joy, Divine Wisdom, Divine Oneness, Divine Tranquility, Divine Humility, Divine Inner Peace, to the center of the planet where every thought will be able to mix with each other and on the way back Harmonize with every molecule on this Planet 100% I AM thanking [Full Birth Name] I AM 24/7 I AM."

Affirmation for Healing the Planet

"I AM placing myself equally spaced around the planet. I invite I AM to move to the center of the planet where every thought will be able to mix with each other and on the way back Harmonize with every molecule on the Planet 100%. I AM entertaining maintaining sustaining and supporting Divine Love Divine Harmony Divine Gratitude Divine forgiveness Divine Light Divine Life Divine Happiness Divine Joy Divine Wisdom Divine Oneness Divine tranquility Divine Humility Divine Inner Peace."

"I invite every molecule on the Planet to come into the light to fulfill their divine destiny throughout your evolutionary thought creation."

Harmony for the Physical Body

"I AM in Harmony with my physical body."

"I AM inviting my thoughts within my cellular DNA, RNA, MICROBES, GENES and the emotional generosity to reactivate the entire self-correcting harmony vibration frequency 100% I AM."

"The efficiency and effectiveness of this Affirmation is 100% and this is throughout my entire life experience I AM [Full Birth Name]."

An Alternative Harmony Affirmation for the Physical Body

"I AM inviting all cellular DNA, RNA/Microbe intelligence vibration frequency within my physical body and throughout my physical life to come into the vibration frequency of Divine Harmony/

Divine Disharmony within the entire metabolism/digestive system of each of my active cellular DNA/RNA, so that the efficiency and effectiveness has been corrected and forever restored to 100% no matter what the circumstances within my physical life experience encounters."

"I AM thanking you, I AM [Full Birth Name]."

Harmony for the Immune System

"My immune system is reaching 100% of my cells to be in harmony balance(s) with disharmonies vibrational frequencies I AM [Full Birth Name]."

"I AM rethinking the efficiency and effectiveness of my cells." [Or whatever you are trying to heal.]

"I AM inviting the interfering thoughts to rethink with me."

"I AM 100% GOD'S CREATION I AM THROUGHOUT MY EVOLUTIONARY THOUGHT CREATION I AM."

Knowledge within Cellular Thoughts

"I AM knowledge I AM."

"I AM every cell within my physical Body I AM 100%."

"I AM dowsing for 100% knowledge within my Cellular thoughts I AM."

"I AM using my thoughts in a different way if every cell is entertaining maintaining sustaining and supporting knowledge 100% throughout our evolutionary God's thoughts creations we will be balancing the Harmony/Disharmony thoughts in a different way I AM."

"I AM [Full Birth Name] I AM."

Self-Correct When Not Feeling Well

"I AM inviting myself to give myself permission to come to the correct vibrational frequency to correct the problem."

"I AM owning and rethinking my [illness] historic limiting thoughts [anything you own doesn't hurt you]."

"There is an activity of [disease] presently active in my physical body."

"I AM rethinking, rethink I AM [Full Birth Name]." ["Rethinking rethink" is reinforcing the thought.]

"I AM inviting thoughts of angels."

"I AM owning and rethinking my thoughts."

"I AM amazing [Full Birth Name]."

"I AM 100% [Full Birth Name]."

"I AM inviting thoughts to rethink with me."

"I AM owning and rethinking my history of addictive limiting thoughts."

"I AM coming into harmony 100% with everything that is."

"My left brain comes together with my right brain with my heart."

"I invite my history of limiting thoughts to come into harmony with disharmony."

"I invite thought forms to come into harmony with disharmony and to rethink the I AM statement."

"I invite myself to come to the correct vibrational frequency of my first thought creation, to correct what needs to be corrected."

"I invite my original soul, mind, and spirit to come back into my body."

Memory or Immune System

The following affirmation can be used for memory/forgetfulness once a day, or for the immune system 3 times a day:

"I AM inviting thoughts within thoughts within thoughts to rethink with me I AM."

"I AM inviting thoughts within thoughts within thoughts within thoughts within thoughts within thoughts to rethink with me I AM."

"I AM inviting thoughts within thoughts within thoughts within thoughts within thoughts within thoughts within thoughts within thoughts within thoughts within thoughts to rethink with me I AM."

Repeating 3 times:

"I AM in Harmony with my thoughts I AM."

"I AM in Harmony with my thoughts I AM."

"I AM in Harmony with my thoughts I AM."

Repeating 6 times:

"I AM in Harmony with my thoughts I AM."

"I AM in Harmony with my thoughts I AM."

"I AM in Harmony with my thoughts I AM."

"I AM in Harmony with my thoughts I AM."

"I AM in Harmony with my thoughts I AM."

"I AM in Harmony with my thoughts I AM."

Repeating 9

"I AM in Harmony with my thoughts I AM."

"I AM in Harmony with my thoughts I AM."

"I AM in Harmony with my thoughts I AM."

"I AM in Harmony with my thoughts I AM."

"I AM in Harmony with my thoughts I AM."

"I AM in Harmony with my thoughts I AM."

"I AM in Harmony with my thoughts I AM."

"I AM in Harmony with my thoughts I AM."

"I AM in Harmony with my thoughts I AM."

Repeating 3 times:

"I AM owning my thoughts I AM."

"I AM owning my thoughts I AM."

"I AM owning my thoughts I AM."

Repeating 6 times:

"I AM owning my thoughts I AM."

"I AM owning my thoughts I AM."

"I AM owning my thoughts I AM."

"I AM owning my thoughts I AM."

"I AM owning my thoughts I AM."

"I AM owning my thoughts I AM."

Repeating 9 times:

"I AM owning my thoughts I AM."

"I AM owning my thoughts I AM."

"I AM owning my thoughts I AM."

"I AM owning my thoughts I AM."

"I AM owning my thoughts I AM."

"I AM owning my thoughts I AM."

"I AM owning my thoughts I AM."

"I AM owning my thoughts I AM."

"I AM owning my thoughts I AM."

———

Repeating 3 times:

"I AM my thoughts I AM."

"I AM my thoughts I AM."

"I AM my thoughts I AM."

Repeating 6 times:

"I AM my thoughts I AM."

"I AM my thoughts I AM."

"I AM my thoughts I AM."

"I AM my thoughts I AM."

"I AM my thoughts I AM."

"I AM my thoughts I AM."

Repeating 9 times:

"I AM my thoughts I AM."

"I AM my thoughts I AM."

"I AM my thoughts I AM."

"I AM my thoughts I AM."

"I AM my thoughts I AM."

"I AM my thoughts I AM."

"I AM my thoughts I AM."

"I AM my thoughts I AM."

"I AM my thoughts I AM."

Repeating 3 times:

"I AM in Harmony with my knowledge I AM."

"I AM in Harmony with my knowledge I AM."

"I AM in Harmony with my knowledge I AM."

Repeating 6 times:

"I AM in Harmony with my knowledge I AM."

"I AM in Harmony with my knowledge I AM."

"I AM in Harmony with my knowledge I AM."

"I AM in Harmony with my knowledge I AM."

"I AM in Harmony with my knowledge I AM."

"I AM in Harmony with my knowledge I AM."

Repeating 9 times:

"I AM in Harmony with my knowledge I AM."

"I AM in Harmony with my knowledge I AM."

"I AM in Harmony with my knowledge I AM."

"I AM in Harmony with my knowledge I AM."

"I AM in Harmony with my knowledge I AM."

"I AM in Harmony with my knowledge I AM."

"I AM in Harmony with my knowledge I AM."

"I AM in Harmony with my knowledge I AM."

"I AM in Harmony with my knowledge I AM."

Repeating 3 times:

"I AM owning my knowledge I AM."

"I AM owning my knowledge I AM."

"I AM owning my knowledge I AM."

Repeating 6 times:

"I AM owning my knowledge I AM."

"I AM owning my knowledge I AM."

"I AM owning my knowledge I AM."

"I AM owning my knowledge I AM."

"I AM owning my knowledge I AM."

"I AM owning my knowledge I AM."

Repeating 9 times:

"I AM owning my knowledge I AM."

"I AM owning my knowledge I AM."

"I AM owning my knowledge I AM."

"I AM owning my knowledge I AM."

"I AM owning my knowledge I AM."

"I AM owning my knowledge I AM."

"I AM owning my knowledge I AM."

"I AM owning my knowledge I AM."

"I AM owning my knowledge I AM."

Repeating 3 times:

"I AM my knowledge I AM."

"I AM my knowledge I AM."

"I AM my knowledge I AM."

Repeating 6 times:

"I AM my knowledge I AM."

"I AM my knowledge I AM."

"I AM my knowledge I AM."

"I AM my knowledge I AM."

"I AM my knowledge I AM."

"I AM my knowledge I AM."

Repeating 9 times:

"I AM my knowledge I AM."

"I AM my knowledge I AM."

"I AM my knowledge I AM."

"I AM my knowledge I AM."

"I AM my knowledge I AM."

"I AM my knowledge I AM."

"I AM my knowledge I AM."

"I AM my knowledge I AM."

"I AM my knowledge I AM."

"I AM self-correcting my evolutionary thoughts creation 100% 24/7 I AM."

"[Full Birth Name] I AM."

"I AM rethinking this wonderful affirmation I AM."

Harmonizing My Memory

"I AM inviting my short term and long term memory to come into harmony with thoughts throughout my evolutionary divine thought creation."

"I AM [Full Birth Name]."

A Healing Affirmation

One of the best healing Affirmations is to RETHINK this:

"I AM the most amazingly delightful thoughts creation I AM."

Please rethink the affirmation 3 times — pause, 6 times — pause, 9 times. Repeat 3 times a day.

For Harmonizing Breath and Regeneration

"I AM regenerating I AM."

Exhale to remove negativity. Repeat 3 times — pause, 6 times — pause — 9 times.

"I AM [Full Birth Name]."

Breathe with emphasis on the exhale. Repeat 3 times - pause, 6 times - pause, 9 times. Then state:

"I AM 100% my own thoughts."

"I AM 100% controlling my own thoughts throughout my evolutionary divine thought creation."

"I AM inviting thoughts within thoughts within thoughts I AM."

Inhale and concentrate on the exhale with this phrase. Repeat phrase 3 times — pause, 6 times — pause, 9 times.

Rethink

"I AM Rethinking — Rethink I AM."

This set of words energetically produces a pause and invites the person to re-evaluate the words of I AM. Knowing you are I AM raises your vibrational level.

"I AM Rethinking — Rethink I AM."

"I AM Rethinking I AM Knowledge I AM."

"I AM Rethinking which Thoughts of my I AM."

"I AM not Controlling I AM."

"I AM giving you permission to think and rethink my harmony affirmation."

Affirmation to Increase Your Vibrational Level (Useful for Dowsers)

Version 1

In addition to enabling you to reach your I AM vibrational level, this affirmation is useful to beginning dowsers whose pendulums or other dowsing tools are not moving on their own. You are your thoughts, so realizing this helps bring a person to the I AM level. By thinking of thoughts within thoughts within thoughts, you are delving deeper and deeper into who you are. In a sense, you are taking a thought journey into the first thoughts of your thought creation.

This affirmation would be used after bringing yourself into harmony by harmonizing your right/left brain and left/right brain with your heart, as described in the Harmony Dowsing affirmation (with women, harmonize left brain/right brain first, then right brain/left brain next).

"I AM inviting thoughts within thoughts to rethink with me and to come to the correct vibration frequency of their first thought creation. I AM [Full Birth Name] I AM."

"Once there,[1] I AM inviting thoughts to come to the correct vibration frequency, where we will be communicating with each other."

Version 2 *(for additional impact)*

To truly reach the vibration frequency of my BELIEF that "I AM Everything I AM," you can repeat the "within thoughts" phrase 3-6-9 times:

3 times:

> "I AM inviting thoughts within thoughts within thoughts within thoughts to rethink with me."

6 times:

> "I AM inviting thoughts within thoughts within thoughts within thoughts within thoughts within thoughts to rethink with me."

9 times:

> "I AM inviting thoughts within thoughts within thoughts within thoughts within thoughts within thoughts within thoughts within thoughts within thoughts to rethink with me and to come to the first vibration frequency of my first thought creation. I AM [Full Birth Name] I AM."

Alternative Harmony and Raising Vibrational Level to the I AM

"I AM the harmony within my disharmony I AM."

Women:

> "I invite my left brain and my right brain to join together with my heart. I invite my right brain and my left brain to join together with my heart I AM."

Men:

> "I invite my right brain and my left brain to join together with my heart. I invite my left brain and my right brain to join together with my heart I AM."

All:

> "I AM rethinking — rethink I AM."

Repeat the above phrase 3 times. Reflect until "I AM 100% I AM."

> "I AM rethinking I AM knowledge I AM."

> "I AM owning my Thoughts I AM.

> "I AM rethinking — rethink I AM."

Repeat the above phrase 3 times. Reflect until "I AM 100% I AM."

"I AM my generosity thoughts I AM.

"I AM rethinking — rethink I AM."

Repeat the above phrase 3 times. Reflect until "I AM 100% I AM."

"I AM owning my Remote Controls[2] I AM.

"I AM rethinking — rethink I AM."

Repeat the above phrase 3 times. Reflect until "I AM 100% I AM."

"I AM my entire I AM Being I AM.

"I AM rethinking — rethink I AM."

Repeat the above phrase 3 times. Reflect until "I AM 100% I AM."

"I AM my evolutionary Divine Thoughts I AM 100% I AM.

"I AM rethinking — rethink I AM."

Repeat this phrase 3 times. Reflect until "I AM 100% I AM."

"I AM [Full Birth Name] I AM.

"I AM inviting all Thoughts to read and rethink this affirmation 10x a day 24/7.

"I AM rethinking — rethink I AM 100% I AM [Full Birth Name] I AM."

Knowledge

"I align myself with Universal Law."

"I AM in balance with Universal Intelligence."

"I AM aligned with thought creation."

"I AM in harmony with Universal Law." [Use if your mind is wandering.]

"I AM opening my door of knowingness."

"I AM inviting greater thoughts to come through in a creative form."

"Mind, go to the Universal Mind, and bring back to me what I need to know for my next step." [Do not stay away longer than 3-5 minutes every hour for 2 hours.]

"I AM knowledge I AM."

"I AM using my thoughts in a different way."

"I AM [Full Birth Name] I AM."

Repeat the above phrase 3 times, 6 times, then 9 times.

"I AM owning and rethinking my limiting thoughts."

"I AM inviting thoughts."

"I AM owning my evolutionary divine thoughts."

"I AM rethinking, rethink I AM." [3x]

"I AM living my evolutionary divine thought creation."

"I AM inviting life to harmonize life."

"Be in harmony with your own dictionary, in harmony with your own thoughts." [You are working with the harmony/disharmony frequency.]

"I AM inviting my conscious mind and my subconscious mind to be in divine harmony."

Spiritual Evolution 1:[3]

"I AM the most amazingly delightful I AM being."

"I AM evolving my spiritual thoughts 100% I AM."

"I AM evolving my emotional thoughts 100% I AM."

"I AM evolving my mental thoughts 100% I AM."

"I AM evolving my physical thoughts 100% I AM."

"I AM rethinking every line 3x, 6x, 9x I AM."

Spiritual Evolution 2:[4]

"I AM the most amazingly delightful I AM being."

"I AM evolving my spiritual thoughts 100% I AM."

"I AM evolving my emotional thoughts 100% I AM."

"I AM evolving my mental thoughts 100% I AM."

"I AM evolving my physical thoughts 100% I AM."

"I AM evolving my immune system thoughts 100% I AM."

"I AM evolving my metabolism thoughts 100% I AM."

"I AM evolving my evolutionary thoughts 100% I AM."

"I AM rethinking every line 3x, 6x, 9x I AM."

Getting a Good Night's Sleep

When you are going to sleep, you can say:

"I'm counting from 1 through 3. By the count of 3, I will be deep asleep."

On 1, say:

"I'm surrounded by the light so that no negativity of any sort will reach or come to me. I'll only accept that which is beneficial for all mankind and myself."

On 2, say:

"I will sleep 8 hours of beautiful, regenerating, harmonious sleep." [Or whatever number of hours you want to sleep.]

On 3, say:

"I'm in deep sleep and will wake up at ____." [Time of your choice.]

"I AM in harmony with my own disharmony."

Repeat:

"I'm rethinking rethink I AM."

Pretty soon you're gone and you are having a wonderful, uninterrupted sleep. If you do this every day, it will come automatically to you.

Summary of Key Points in This Chapter

It has been an amazing experience getting to know Joachim, be friends, and learn from him. He has taught the essence of healing, which is coming into harmony with the disharmony and coming into the essence of I AM. In this chapter, we have learned many pearls of wisdom from Joachim. Each pearl is unique and well worth reading and understanding. Joachim's affirmations are wonderful in bringing you into harmony, realizing that you are your thoughts, and rethinking your true I AM essence.

The keys to Joachim's teachings are:

- Achieving Harmony (affirmations, inviting in harmony).
- We are our thoughts and need to pay attention to our thoughts.
- Achieving our I AM level to truly connect with who we are and be at that higher level of vibration and balance. We learned some affirmations to help us achieve this level of vibration.

Notes

[1] "Once there" refers to being at the thought level of the first thought creation. With the thought journey to the first thought creation, thoughts have encountered all the thoughts from the first thought creation. This allows the full understanding of creation and I AM. The "Once there..." phrase can be read out loud or silently, or mentally thought and understood.

[2] The term "Remote Controls" refers to those words, thoughts, and statements that cause an emotional, gut reaction from you. It is those words that "push your button."

[3] and [4] "Spiritual Evolution" refers to how fast a person wants to progress in his/her spiritual growth.

CHAPTER 12

Journey of a Seeker

My driving interest has always been to gain a better understanding of the nature of the universe and the nature of who I am.

Since this book is based on what I learned about spirit and healing (especially from Joachim Wippich), I want to share my journey with you in three parts:

1. A short section on my early years,
2. A description of my years as a businessman and scientist, and
3. My journey as a spiritual seeker.

My Early Years

From a young age, my driving interest has been to gain a better understanding of the nature of the universe and the nature of who I am. Synchronicity—the simultaneous occurrence of events that appear significantly related but have no discernible causal connection—has led me on an amazing journey, especially in the last 17 years. It appears that synchronicity is how our guides and the divine work with us to help us manifest our reality.

For example, when I was only about nine, I had the task of helping my mother take a train from Tucson, Arizona to San Francisco, California. She spoke no English and could not read, and we would have to change trains. The night before we were to take the train, I came up with the intention that we would sit by someone who could help guide us. It turned out that a Chinese gentleman sat next to us and guided us throughout the trip.

My life has been a continuous sequence of synchronicities happening at all the crucial moments. Reflecting back reveals that I have always followed my intuition for my basic decisions, even though I never thought about synchronicity until the last ten years.

Synchronicity and Science

I have always had an interest in science and how everything is put together. In my junior year of high school in Tucson, I had a superior chemistry teacher, Mr. Bazzetta, who instilled in me a love for chemistry. It was the time when the Soviet Union put Sputnik, the first satellite, into space. This caused the US to realize that it was behind in the space race, and that science needed to be emphasized in schools.

Thus, the first advanced placement course in chemistry would be taught at our high school. At the end of the course, we would take the same tests given at the University of Arizona to see if we were eligible for college credit for chemistry. I took the course, and loved the field. This set me on the path to major in chemistry at the University of Arizona.

The chemistry of *life* was what interested me; I was fascinated by its study. At that time, Watson and Crick came out with their deciphering of the mechanism on how DNA worked. In my final year in college, as part of studying the chemistry of life, I took Biochemistry, which the University of Arizona offered for the very first time. I loved that course so very much that it set the stage for me to decide to go to graduate school to become a biochemist.

So by this time, synchronicity (or divine guidance) had led me to:

- The field of chemistry,
- The first advanced placement course in chemistry, and
- The first biochemistry course taught at the University of Arizona.

It even determined whom I would marry.

Synchronicity and Marriage

The summer before entering college, I had spent time playing the junior tennis circuit with my high school friend and tennis team doubles partner. We ended up placing third nationally in the interscholastic doubles, and had a decent ranking in the national junior doubles. That was the year I won the Southwest Tennis Tournament and became the top-ranked junior player in that region.

At the end of that summer, I traveled to San Francisco to join my mother, who was staying with my sister and her husband. My mother was to attend the wedding of a friend from Tucson who was marrying a lady from San Francisco. However, *I* was going to San Francisco for a different reason: to play in the National Chinese Tennis Tournament.

After the first day of the tournament, I met up with another tennis player to go to a party at his friend's house. There, across the room, I saw a beautiful young lady dancing with another gentleman. When he left to get snacks, I introduced myself; her name was Peggy. While we danced, I asked if she wanted to go out the following day. She said she could go out—but only after a wedding party she was going to attend was over, since she was a bridesmaid.

It turned out that the person who was getting married was Peggy's sister, and that the groom was from Tucson. In short, it was the very wedding that my mother came to San Francisco to attend.

Synchronicity!

After I returned to Tucson, Peggy and I corresponded by letter and saw each other on holidays.

Synchronicity and Graduate Work in Biochemistry

After three years of college and making up my mind to become a biochemist, I needed to find a university where I could study for a PhD in biochemistry. My undergraduate work had been paid by scholarships, and I needed a source of funding for graduate school. My parents owned a small restaurant in Tucson, and they wouldn't have money to send me to graduate school. I needed another way.

After I applied to various schools, the University of California at Berkeley accepted my application, and offered me a US Public Health Traineeship. This would be enough to pay for tuition and housing.

And, Peggy would be just across the Bay in San Francisco. Synchronicity!

Peggy and I got married after my first year in graduate school.

After four years, I got my PhD. This was the time of the Free Speech Movement, which started at Berkeley. The movement was aimed at the draft of young men who had no interest in fighting a war in Viet Nam. My deferrals for education were over, and I would be drafted as soon as the PhD was awarded. I too had no interest in fighting in Viet Nam.

Synchronicity and Not Fighting in Viet Nam

I learned that another PhD from Berkeley, Dr. Edith Miles, had a lab at the National Institutes of Health in Bethesda. She would be able to accept a postdoc—*if* the person could be funded. So I checked into joining the Public Health Service with the intent of working for Dr. Miles. It turned out that the Public Health Service would take care of my two years of the draft — I became the equivalent of a US Navy Lieutenant. Synchronicity strikes again!

Early Seeds of Synchronicity

During this time, I started playing tennis with Dr. Vernon Wong, a prominent ophthalmologist researcher/clinician at the National Eye Institute. This was another point of synchronicity, which would manifest years later.

Entering the Field of Laboratory Medicine

Our first son Rodney was born at the US Naval Hospital in Bethesda. I knew I would have to find a place of employment after my two years of being a postdoc. There were very few jobs for biochemists. An academic career was typical in this profession, but that would take many years of being a postdoc at various institutions until an opening occurred.

Since pay as a postdoc was very low (at that time, only about $8,000/year) and I now had a family, I figured that working in the field of laboratory medicine would make sense. A biochemist knows chemistry in relation to chemical reactions, but has no knowledge of the clinical, diagnostic, and medical applications. Thus, I knew I would have to learn a new field.

My Business Years in the Science Field

I looked up the major clinical labs in the country and sent a letter to BioScience Labs in Van Nuys, California. They wrote back and said they wanted to interview me. At that time, BioScience was just initiating a training program for future Directors, since they had a plan to expand throughout the US. This was an ideal situation. Synchronicity!

I worked as an Acting Assistant Director and learned the fields of clinical chemistry, endocrinology, immunology, microbiology, hematology, and toxicology. During that time, our second son, Brian, was born. BioScience, which was owned by Dow Chemical, wanted to set up their first Branch Lab in New York. I was selected to set up the lab as Assistant Director, in Rockville Centre, Long Island.

After setting up the lab, BioScience decided to have me set up another branch in Columbia, Maryland, so I became the Director of the Baltimore/Washington Branch of BioScience Labs. As Director, I was now also a business guy, responsible for the bottom line and needing to bring in business, and to know about income statements and marketing.

I had no choice but to learn this field. I thus spent my evenings and weekends at Loyola College in Baltimore to earn an MBA.

After I got the MBA, Dow Chemical moved me to Midland, Michigan, to become a Corporate Product Director in the fields of pharmaceuticals, diagnostics, and consumer products.

As Corporate Product Director, I learned about the world, since the job entailed connecting the businesses throughout the world — Latin America, US, Canada, Europe, and Asia. About 50 percent of the time I was traveling internationally. After this tenure, Dow moved me to become Director of International Diagnostics in Indianapolis.

After about a year in this capacity, Dow decided to sell their pharmaceutical and diagnostic businesses and just concentrate on their core chemical business. Their BioScience Labs got sold. (It is now known as Quest Labs — the largest clinical lab in the US.)

An Entrepreneur in the Science Field

At this point in my career, my thinking was to become an entrepreneur. But in what field? Synchronicity again came into play to move me to the heart of the biotech industry. I sent out my resume and had an interview with Syva, the diagnostic arm of Syntex Pharmaceuticals in Palo Alto, California. I was hired, and I became their Director of Strategic Planning and New Business Development.

In addition to helping Syva in their planning, in the process I learned another new field—the growing area of biotechnology.

Home Cholesterol Testing: After five years at Syva, I met with some researcher-friends who wanted to start a company. I convinced them that the field of home cholesterol testing would become big, and that we should develop a simple home cholesterol test in a stick format.

This was again synchronicity, since I had spent a lot of time on the Dow cholesterol-lowering drug business and knew that a lot of attention would be paid to cholesterol testing. The focus on educating doctors had not occurred yet, since doctors and clinicians only looked at the normal range of cholesterol as their guide.

Since in the US population's cholesterol was high, the range considered normal was high. Thus, a doctor would not be concerned about a value of 250 mg/dl, since so many persons had high cholesterol levels. This, however, would change when the National Institutes of Health started their national education programs to revise this mindset.

At this time, my two researcher-friends and I were all working in comfortable jobs. To get our new company moving forward, one of us had to leave the job and raise money. So to make this happen, I left Syva; and after about six months, I had raised our first million dollars of venture money to get our company, ChemTrak, formed. Prithipal Singh, one of the two friends, then left his job to become President, and I became Vice President. The third friend was in another startup at that time and could not join our team.

After five years of research and development, our "Accumeter" was approved by the FDA as the first quantitative home cholesterol test from a drop of a finger-pricked blood. The company had its initial public offering. Then, after a few more years, the company was sold.

Starting Two Other Companies—Visionex and Oculex Pharmaceuticals: As I was leaving Syva, I only had enough money in the bank to pay my mortgage for about six months. Not wanting to leave things to chance, I had also started two other companies.

My friend Dr. Vernon Wong, from my days at Bethesda, Maryland, wanted to develop drug delivery for the inside of the eye. I decided to partner with him. My thought was that if our product would take many years to develop, it would be good to develop a *simpler* product that could be a source of faster income.

After some discussions, I figured I could make a simpler and easier-to-use Schirmer Tear Test for testing dry eyes. I developed the technology, applied for a patent, learned how to make the product, and applied for FDA approval as a medical device. Upon approval, we started selling the product in our new company, Visionex, and eventually found a distributor for it, as well as a contract manufacturer. My wife Peggy continues to run that company to this day.

Ozurdex: Vernon and I then spent the next ten years developing our drug-delivery product for the inside of the eye. We took whatever money we made from ChemTrak (Vernon privately invested in ChemTrak when we started the company) and plowed it into Oculex Pharmaceuticals. The venture community told us that no one would ever want to inject a drug/delivery system into the eye. Thus, we had to develop the product through Phase I Clinical Trials with our own money.

All the major ophthalmic companies had the same opinion as the venture community — that no one would inject a drug delivery product directly into the eye. Once more, we were down to our last month of personal money to keep the company going, when synchronicity/serendipity again came into play: I met with a venture capitalist from Singapore, who brought us to the head of the National Eye Institute in Singapore.

Our product was a biodegradable delivery system about the size of a grain of salt for delivering a steroid into the eye. It would be perfect for use after cataract surgery. The head of the National Eye Institute (NEI) said he liked the concept and the results from a few patients we had tested. He agreed to do clinical trials on our product, and we got funding from the Singapore venture company.

In the world of pharmaceuticals, many rounds of funding are needed, and multiple venture companies become involved. After ten years of hard work, with a year left in completing Phase II Clinical Trials, the venture groups succeeded in taking over the company and diluted ownership with the non-deep-pocket initial investors as well as founders.

At the completion of Phase II clinicals for macular edema, the company was sold to Allergan. By then, based on our work, all the ophthalmic companies understood the value of a drug delivery system for the inside of the eye: eye drops cannot penetrate there, making diseases of the retina difficult to treat.

The company was sold to Allergan, which would use our technology to develop their future drugs for the inside of the eye.

Our product is in the market and is sold by Allergan as "Ozurdex." The inside-of-the-eye drug delivery market is now a billion-dollar industry.

Nuvora (Sustained-Release Lozenge Technology): In 2003, with Oculex Pharmaceuticals now behind us, Ben (my head of Manufacturing Development at Oculex) and I asked ourselves about the key needs in medicine, in terms of drug delivery. We determined that the ability to have drug delivery through the oral mucosa was an area that was inadequately developed.

And so we formed Nuvora, and spent the next four years working in my home lab to develop the sustained-release lozenge technology. We wanted to get into the cough/cold segment but lacked an appropriate new drug for that application.

Working with some dental friends who recommended that we go after the dry-mouth market, we developed "Salese," a lozenge for long-lasting relief of dry mouth. Salese gives longer relief for dry mouth than any other product. It contains ingredients not only for the relief of dry mouth, but also for reducing bacteria levels in the mouth, neutralizing acids (which cause cavities), and capturing volatile sulfur compounds (which cause bad breath).

Simultaneously, we developed "Dentiva," an oral-health and breath-freshening lozenge that eliminates bad breath, reduces acidity in the mouth to prevent cavities, and reduces bacteria in the mouth. It has the same ingredients as Salese, but without the ingredient for dry mouth. It is probably the best lozenge in the market for bad breath. The zinc in the lozenge not only captures odor-causing volatile sulfur compounds, but also can coat the oral mucosa as an aid for colds and other viral infections.

Livionex Dental Gel: At the same time that we were developing Nuvora, two other friends had discovered a way to get eye drops to penetrate into the eye. Since they were not ophthalmologists, they wanted to know what application should be developed for this technology. With my experience at Oculex, I had some ideas. My two friends, Rajiv and Amit, and I thus formed Chakshu and focused on development of an eye drop that would help dissolve early cataracts, enabling people to have improved vision as they got older.

We obtained some venture funding, developed the product, and proceeded to carry out clinical trials. Our placebo was artificial tears. But what we did not realize was that in an older population, people suffer from dry eyes, and that artificial tears will also improve vision. As a result, we improved two lines of vision but not three lines. We could repeat the trials and correct for the placebo effect, but that would cost another $20 million. The venture groups would not back that, so we took back the patent and decided on another application that we could self-fund.

We thus formed Livionex and developed our Livionex Dental Gel, the best toothpaste on the market by several orders of magnitude. This product can also treat gingivitis and periodontitis, but that will take additional FDA approved clinical trials. We plan to do that. In the meantime, the Livionex Dental Gel is on the market. We also have a broad-based metal modulation technology that will result in many key products in the future.

My Spiritual Journey

When Oculex Pharmaceuticals was sold to Allergan in 2003, I was 60. This was the age when my spiritual life journey began.

Finding My Way Outside of Formal Religion

Growing up, my family had practiced no formal religions. Mom would observe some Buddhist traditions by burning incense at an altar, chanting prayers, and eating vegetarian dishes on certain days. But we were never taught the meaning of any of this, other than these traditions needed to be done.

At the same altar, there was a picture of Christ, so the praying was meant for the avatars who would be beneficial. We never went to any church, so we were never taught any formal religion. However, I wanted to understand religion, since almost everyone I knew except our family went to church and practiced their religions.

So at age 12, I started reading the Bible, checked out books that described both the Old and New Testaments, practically memorized *The Greatest Story Ever Told*, and memorized the Lord's Prayer.

On my own, I became very religious, but I could not reconcile the teachings in the Bible. These teachings talked about souls who could not go to heaven unless they believed (that is, in Christ). Since I knew that more than half the population of Earth was not Christian, this meant that much of the world was therefore condemned.

I felt this was inherently wrong, so I stepped away from the typical Western beliefs and started reading about the great religions of the world. Eventually, I realized that all religions said about the same thing: one had to be morally good and loving. I accepted that philosophy as my way of life and did not pay much more attention to religion. By then, I was around 14 years of age.

The Pull to the Esoteric

In spite of the formal exposure to religions, there was always a pull to the spiritual and esoteric topics. I devoured the ESP work by J. B. Rhine, the American parapsychologist who coined the term "extrasensory perception."

When I was in graduate school at Berkeley, I learned about Transcendental Meditation. This intrigued me, so I signed up with a teacher who explained about meditation in an hour or two, then sat me down and gave me a mantra to repeat for about 20 minutes.

The meditation was amazing in how it quieted the mind. The 20 minutes went by as if there was no time. I practiced that meditation over the years on a sporadic basis, because life was always busy. In the work world after my post-doc years, my time was devoted to family and work, with not much time to spend on the meaning of life.

Discovering Energies

At the age of 50, my lower back was bothering me, so I decided to go to a yoga class. My partner at work said his wife knew a good yoga teacher, Guy Harriman. Thus, synchronicity sent me to Guy. This would change my life.

Guy was into the world of energies, and had an understanding of yoga, qi gong, and subtle energies. The yoga class was in his home, which had five or six huge quartz crystals.

We started our yoga class with some warm-up qi gong exercises. In the first exercise, we moved our hands to build up energy and then put the palms of the hands facing each other at the chest and at the *dan tian* area below the navel. We were told to hold the palms in that position to feel the central column of *qi*, which would grow to feel like a weight.

I went through the motions, not expecting to feel anything. To my amazement, my hands began to buzz/tingle and I let the energy build. It became a force that became substantial, penetrating into my hands. This was truly amazing! My scientific career had never prepared me for this!

Another qi gong exercise was to build up the qi and send it to the world as a prayer.

After the class, I spoke to the other students and asked what they felt when they were doing the qi gong exercises. Did they feel the "energy"? The other students did not feel what I felt. Guy explained to me that different people had different sensitivities to energy, and that with practice, sensitivities would grow.

Since he knew I could feel the energies, he brought me over to the large quartz crystals and had me hold my hand above them. To my amazement, my hands began to "tingle," the signal indicating that I was feeling the energy. Guy then placed a small rock containing quartz into the palm of my hand, and rotated his palm over my palm. The quartz took on a life of its own, and I started to feel as if it was vibrating.

Being a curious scientist, I had to *learn* about the energies I was feeling. What was it that I felt? I decided to read everything I could find about "energies." I wanted to look at the science books first. James Oschman's book *Energy Medicine in Therapeutics & Human Performance* was excellent and forward-thinking on the biochemistry of energy and the human condition. Richard Gerber described *Vibrational Medicine*, and Michael Talbot discussed *The Holographic Universe*. These and other excellent books had new and important information; but from a scientific basis, nothing truly explained what I was feeling in terms of energy and what all this energy stuff was all about.

Seeing Energies: As a scientist, I thought that if I could *feel* energy, could I also *see* it? I had heard about auras and wondered if that was what I felt. Since I was feeling the central column of qi between my palms, I wondered if I could see that.

I put my palms about a foot in front of my face, and looked through the empty space between them as I moved them up and down. This was done in front of a blank wall. To my surprise, I saw lines of "energy" between my palms. Some people would call it "smoke," but I could see the connections between my palm and fingers, which to me looked like lines.

In the evening, lying in bed, I wondered if I could see the "energy" of prayer, which Guy described as a beam being sent out into the world. I held my palm up and, to my surprise, there was a beam of energy going from my hand clear across the room! If I pointed my finger, similarly there was a beam, which went across the room. However, I was not seeing the colored auras that clairvoyants often see around people. I did see a "layer" next to the skin, which I later learned was the etheric layer.

Seeing "Rays": Now that I was sensitized to seeing "energies," I started to look at people. On a cloudy day, I could see "rays" above the head of a person. I then noticed these same rays above everyone's heads as I looked at them.

One day at the gym, I was looking at a person going up and down on the StairMaster, and decided to follow the rays from the person's head to see where they would go. There seemed to be a "shadow" several meters above the head that moved up and down as the person went up and down. This was consistent with anyone I saw on the StairMaster. Later, I was to learn more about the subtle bodies, and found out that this "shadow" might be their mental body.

My next question was, "What is the purpose or utility of the energies I am seeing?" I was wondering if they might be useful in healing. By this time, I also realized that there was nothing in the standard scientific/medical realm that would give me information on what I was seeing and feeling. If I wanted to learn about energies and healing, I would need to go to all the healers and learn from them. I knew from my medical and scientific background that experience and practice would be the only real teachers.

Learning from Healers

As a result, I attended every healing workshop that came into my awareness. I went through Matrix Energetics by Richard Bartlett, studied Eric Pearl's reconnection method, learned Richard Gordon's Quantum Touch, the Yuen Method, Jane Katra's spiritual healing, and Reiki. I learned about cycling from Bill Bengston, attended teachings by shamans, observed and experienced the healing of Eliza Mada Dalian, author of *Healing the Body & Awakening Consciousness with the Dalian Method: An Advanced Self-Healing System for a New Humanity*; learned many techniques from Caroline Cory, and learned about sound healing, Body Talk, and various other modalities.

It turns out that *all* healing modalities work. The teachers and students could all heal, but no one truly understood how the healing was occurring. Typically, energetic connection with a person takes place—whether by touch or at a distance—and healing occurs. Healing is not based on a specific "thing" that the healer does. My deepest understanding of healing would come from Joachim Wippich later in my journey.

Developing My Own Style of Healing

As I was still a business entrepreneur and scientist/researcher, I could practice healing on family and friends only sporadically, when they allowed me to work on them. I developed my own style of healing, based on a blend of the techniques I had learned. With practice, I found that I could "feel" the presence of a problem/inflammation, since the area needing healing typically has a "buzzing/tingling" feel. As I give "energy/connection" to the problem, the problem goes away on its own. As the problem resolves, my experience of the tingling sensation suddenly goes away, signaling the completion of the healing.

My healing methods would continue to evolve after learning about BioGeometry, about the modality used by Joachim, and the new knowledge I have been calling 3-6-9.

Over the next several years, my understanding evolved further, including learning from various lectures and books. I enjoyed visiting various bookstores, but my favorite was the EastWest Bookstore in Mountain View, California. Intuition/synchronicity would lead me to the shelf holding the next book to read for my evolving growth, as well as to the next lecture at EastWest.

The Foundation for Mind-Being Research (FMBR)

Prior to all that, a friend had introduced me to the Foundation for Mind-Being Research (FMBR). The organization had more science-based members than I had encountered to this point, and gave monthly lectures on a wide range of topics. I became a regular attendee. A few years into my attending lectures, Bill Gough, the founder of FMBR, approached me and asked if I would attend a Board meeting. I said okay, since I really liked the organization.

By then Bill was questioning whether to keep the organization going, since it was a lot of work and strictly dependent on volunteers. There was always only a few thousand dollars in the coffers to keep the organization going. Attendees Judy Kitt and Mary Cummings were also asked to attend that Board meeting. The three of us were invited to become Board members, and we all accepted.

In the midst of this timeframe, Bill Gough said he would transition to being CEO Emeritus. Edie Fischer, the current Chair, said that she would transition to being just a Board member. She and Bill asked if I would be chairman/CEO. Judy Kitt was asked to be President, and

Mary Cummings was asked to be Vice President in charge of Programs. We had a new team.

FMBR has brought many lecturers to teach a wide range of topics—from healing, quantum physics, remote viewing, channeling, electronic communications with those on the other side, sacred geometry, out-of-body experiences, near-death experiences, new ways to look at biology, and many other amazing fields. On my spiritual journey, FMBR allowed me to meet and get to know many scientists and leaders in the broad and wonderful field of mind-being.

I have already told the story in Chapter 1 about Edie Fischer teaching a group of us how to bend spoons into a pretzel shape at a spoon-bending party. This showed that most people have this ability — that we are all more than we believe we are, and that we all have the ability to affect the nature of matter. Since dowsing was what we used to help us discover our ability, I was thus introduced into the wonderful world of dowsing and the ability to tap into information from the right brain.

Dowsing and the San Jose Dowsers

As a consequence of the spoon-bending party, I learned about the San Jose Dowsers, which met monthly. I read books about dowsing and learned more from the experts at the San Jose Dowsers. There were always two instructors who taught for free. One taught dowsing, and the other taught the use of dowsing for healing purposes. I eagerly learned from both instructors.

The San Jose Dowsers also helped host the annual West Coast Dowsers Conference in Santa Cruz, which gave me a chance to meet some very gifted dowsers, such as Walt Woods who wrote the popular (and free) *Letter to Robin*, instructing beginners how to dowse (*see* Chapter 8, "Dowsing, Harmony, and the Vibrational Level"). I invited Walt to give a lecture at FMBR and he taught us dowsing and much more.

Meeting Joachim Wippich

Being a member of the San Jose Dowsers, I have known Joachim Wippich for many years. He has been the teacher of dowsing for healing for the San Jose Dowsers for the past eight years. I listened to his talks on Harmonic Dowsing and was fascinated by his concepts. As we chatted over the years, I learned about his profound understanding of Harmony and I AM. His thoughts and my understandings from being a Seeker merged. We became close friends and have had many discussions, which have expanded our understanding of the nature of everything, especially ourselves. His influence on my spiritual life was deeply important, as the earlier parts of this book make clear. We meet and talk at the monthly FMBR lectures; at the monthly San Jose Dowsers meetings and lectures; at my monthly Study Group Meetings for FMBR; and at his Saturday coffee shop gatherings, where he imparts healing, harmony, and helps bring people to learn and reach their I AM level. In recent years, Joachim and I often gather at my home, where we have amazing discussions on many topics ranging from the nature of everything to current research activities on the same subject.

Learning About Sacred Geometry, the History of Mankind, and the MerKaBa

Around the same timeframe, as I was browsing in the EastWest Bookstore, intuition/synchronicity led me to pick up the *Flower of Life* books by Drunvalo Melchizedek. These books introduced me to a number of important areas — sacred geometry, an alternative history of mankind, and the formation of the MerKaBa.

From sacred geometry, I learned how fundamental geometric structures were embedded in all matter, and were basic to the creation of matter. This was a new view, not taught by traditional science. For me, as a chemist, this was *revolutionary* news, though it had been known by the ancients more than 10,000 years ago.

Then there was the history of mankind. In school we were taught about Darwin and evolution. Religions have their version of the creation. However, Melchizedek added a whole other perspective on the matter. He described the visit of the Annunaki, who came to Earth to mine gold to protect their own world from loss of their atmosphere 500,000 years ago. After many years of doing the hard work of mining, the decision was made to carry out genetic modification of intelligent apes, combining their DNA with the DNA from the Annunaki. Thus, the first Adam was born.

This story was described by Zecharia Sitchin in his *Earth Chronicles* series of books. The story was pieced together by Sitchin's translation of the ancient Sumerian cuneiform writings on clay tablets, written around 4000 BC. The cosmology of how Earth was formed and the locations of all the planets rotating around the sun were described in the ancient writings, long before Western science figured out the structure of the solar system, and way before the planet Pluto was ever discovered.

The third piece of information that I gained from the *Flower of Life* books was the knowledge of the MerKaBa. The MerKaBa is created by the spinning of the sets of tetrahedrons (forming a star tetrahedron, or Star of David structure) that surround each of us. It is considered a light body, and can house our consciousness and aid in our ascension.

I was quite intrigued by this structure and wanted to learn how to form the MerKaBa, so I looked up local teachers and found Ilizabeth Fortune. Ilizabeth is a very talented, intuitive lady; she was featured in the *Flower of Life* book as the person who spoke with the dolphins. My wife Peggy and I spent two days in Ukiah with Ilizabeth, learning the experiential MerKaBa exercises. At her ranch, we learned to speak with her horses — who are equally very intuitive.

Having learned that I could heal others, bend spoons, form a MerKaBa, and see energy lines, I began to really want to understand the nature of myself and everyone else. *Everyone* seemed to have these abilities — they just did not know that they were much more than just physical beings. Thus, I was led to search into the areas of enlightenment and the practice of yogis.

I had read David Hawkins' book, *Power vs. Force,* where he realized that you could tell truth from falsehood by means of kinesiology. Hawkins created an exponential scale from zero to 1000 to measure the level of enlightenment of people. A person in the levels below 200 typically lived in the realm of fear and anger; educated persons, such as those in the US, were in the range of 400; 500 and above was the dividing line, where people realized that there is more than just the physical universe, and that there is a higher level that we could call God; and at the very top of the scale were the great avatars such as Christ.

I had read David's journey from being a very successful psychiatrist to his disillusionment and his search for enlightenment. David taught what one has to go through to reach enlightenment in his books and DVDs, all of which I read and listened to with avid interest. I learned the key lessons of "no judgment, compassion, forgiveness, and love" in a much deeper way than just hearing the words. Some of his other books and CDs include: *The Eye of the I; I — Reality and Subjectivity; Truth vs. Falsehood; In the World but Not of It;* and *The Highest Level of Enlightenment.*

Learning Who We Really Are from Caroline Cory

The next step in my spiritual journey came when I attended a lecture by Caroline Cory at the EastWest Bookstore. I bought and read her first three books: *The Visible & Invisible Worlds of God, God Among Us,* and *The Divine Plan Beyond 2012.* Her books resonated with me, so when she offered a Masters Course to discover who we really are, I decided to enroll. Caroline has an amazing way to lead one to the truth. She would teach a spiritual or healing concept, then lead us in a meditation to reach and observe for ourselves the nature of her teachings.

I had an amazing experience in one meditation when we were led to experience Source Energy, in which I found myself in a brilliant luminescent space of white light with tinges of green. We were taught many concepts, along with experiential meditations, concerning the energies and beings who work with us and with the universe. A variety of healing modalities were also taught. One modality I found successful for me was in recognizing a color of light that a person needed for healing, and to give that colored light to the person. Caroline's teachings were definitely a step in the right direction toward my quest for enlightenment.

Learning Enlightenment from Mada Eliza Dalian

Another very important step in my spiritual journey was meeting Mada Eliza Dalian. She had studied with her guru, Osho, in India and had reached enlightenment. I enjoyed her book, *In Search of the*

Miraculous: Healing into Consciousness, and I had heard her talk at EastWest Bookstore. I had read her materials on enlightenment and understood the left-brain concepts of it, but I wanted the inner knowing and a true understanding about who we are, and who I am. Mada had reached this stage, so when she gave a workshop in Canada, I decided to attend and speak with her. I was in for an amazing adventure.

The workshop with Mada was excellent; she is intuitive and can see people's problems and help them overcome those problems. But I wanted more, so I booked a healing session with her for myself. At the session, I told her that I was not interested in healing but wanted to know more about the process of reaching enlightenment. Her immediate reply was, "You will reach enlightenment. Don't worry about it. Tell me about any physical problems you have."

I told her that sometimes I have a heart arrhythmia, which can be inconvenient if I am playing in a tennis tournament. She told me to lie down on the massage table. Mada concentrated for a few moments, and then said, "The problem does not have to do with you. It has a lineage that goes back to many generations of your ancestors." At that point, I immediately knew the nature of the problem. It was the fear of death.

In our household, growing up, we were taught never to say the number "four," since in Chinese this word sounds like "death." Thus, we never spoke about death or the dead. I explained this to Mada. She then told me that I should release the fear for all the generations of my deceased ancestors: to breathe and release the fear through my feet. As I started to breathe, amazing energies began to flow through my body and my feet. My breathing became heavier, and more and more energy flowed out from my body through my feet.

After maybe about ten minutes of this huge energy flow, it ceased; and I knew that we had succeeded in clearing this fear from those who had died years before. Now I did not have to carry this fear into future generations. When I got up from the massage table, my voice had completely changed and I felt so light. When I went back to my hotel room, Peggy immediately said to me, "You have changed."

A few years later, Mada came to FMBR to give a lecture. She stayed at our home. Mada had developed a new way to lead people to heal on their own, the "Dalian Method." It was a wonderful book that taught people to recognize the underlying cause of their problems. I had read the book but had not practiced the exercises. Mada said I should do the exercises in the book and that she could coach me through it. I said, "Okay."

As we went through the exercises, it became clear that I still had a blockage. I was sad that, being a boy in a family of girls (five sisters), I was always treated better than the girls. I felt it was unfair to them. This was the Chinese cultural way — boys were always first. I needed to overcome the unease and unfairness of being treated better, and to understand it as an adult.

The exercises Mada had me go through allowed me to come to grips with my feelings from childhood. It was a huge release for me. At the end of the session, Mada asked me a question, which she said she never asked of others, but would ask me because she thought I was ready. The question was: "Who are you?" I knew the answer; it was, "I AM."

My Quest to Understand the Nature of the Universe

Part of my quest for enlightenment had an element of wanting to understand the nature of the universe. I understood the standard sciences of biology, chemistry, physics, and medicine, but none of that answers the true nature of creation and how and why things are put together.

My reading had now extended to quantum physics and books such as Michael Talbot's *The Holographic Universe*. I enjoyed books such as Norman Friedman's *Bridging Science and Spirit*, which included Nobel Prize-winning physicist Niels Bohr's descriptions of the materialization of the physical world from the implicate realm to the explicate realm where we live.

A big step forward in my understanding occurred when I discovered a very interesting website, DivineCosmos.com, by David Wilcock. I read all his writings on the website and found it fascinating. For the first time, I heard explanations of the many mysteries of the universe and of consciousness. What I learned from Wilcock in the Divine Cosmos website would later come out in his best-selling book, *Source Field Investigations*.

Through his teachings, I learned about the Source Field and the wondrous things that happen in it. There was Cleve Backster, proving that communications with plants is real by using lie-detector technology. There were experiments using light and sound to incorporate duck characteristics into chickens by passing duck information into chicken eggs. Similar experiments were carried out with salamanders and frogs.

I learned about the mysteries of the pyramids; of levitation used by Tibetan monks; of rainbow bodies when Tibetan monks decided to pass on and change their bodies into light; of healing at a distance; of a piece of metal losing weight when struck with a hammer and regaining that weight a short time later; of how matter can soften in a tornado to allow straw to penetrate wood; of the nature of space-time and its conversion to time-space under the right conditions; and so on.

Wilcock talked about our destinies being guided by a hidden intelligence — "a living energy field the entire Universe is built from." He wrote, "Since this force may be the source of all space, time, matter, energy, biology and consciousness in the Universe, the simplest all-inclusive term I use is the Source Field."

Two other wonderful resources on understanding this field are given by Ervin Laszlo in his book *Science and the Akashic Field*, and by Lynne McTaggart in her book, *The Field*.

Around 2010, synchronicity introduced me to the works of Walter Russell, who lived from the late 19th century to the early 1960s. Russell was a polymath with skills in many fields. He was a national figure-skating champion, a renowned painter and sculptor of key pieces displayed in Washington, D.C., and a musician. His talents came from the Divine — he would meditate to bring in the skills needed for any project. He took annual retreats into the woods to mediate and converse with God.

In his two-volume book, *The Message of the Divine Iliad*, Russell described how he went into a trance and God, in a flash, gave him the explanation of how all things were created and centered by God. In this altered state, his *The Divine Iliad* was channeled and written within the next 40 days.

The more technical details of the working of creation are explained in his book, *The Universal One*. For those seeking a greater understanding of his work and a higher state of enlightenment — which he calls "becoming a cosmic man" — he and his wife put together *The Home Course*, which contains ten booklets to be read and understood over a period of a year.

The key message from Walter Russell is that creation is accomplished by weaving light to create matter, and its de-creation is accomplished by radiating it out, from there to be recycled back into matter again. Creation thus occurs in repeating waves/cycles. Light is divided into polar "male" and "female" aspects (blue and red) and compressed centripetally in clockwise spirals to form matter, then disintegrated/radiated centrifugally in counterclockwise spirals.

The waves of creation and de-creation occur continuously. Thus, matter is formed and broken down, but consciousness is eternal. It all comes back to the Oneness of God everywhere, and that we are not separate from God. Ultimately, it is the story of the I AM and the progression of man to that understanding. The periodic table created by Walter Russell, using his theories, predicted new elements that were later validated.

In my spiritual journey, understanding Walter Russell's work has been key to my further understanding of how everything is put together and who we are, the I AM. All the pieces fit together, from the spiritual to the basic concepts of creation. The work of Nassim Haramein, as well as the understandings from Foster Gamble and Arthur Young (all described below), fit in the I AM puzzle. As described in Chapter 6, "I AM," it is all simple, yet profound.

Understanding Walter Russell's concept is important for further understanding of matter formation as discussed by Nassim Haramein in his DVD, *Crossing the Event Horizon: Rise to the Equation*, when he talks about the torus and double torus as fundamental to creation of everything, from the micro (atomic size) to the macro (the galaxies). The torus structure is basically the movement of energy into the center (creation) and back out (de-creation). Much of

Haramein's teachings can be found at his Resonance Science Foundation, *https://www.resonancescience.org/*

Foster Gamble, a writer and film producer who glimpsed what he perceived to be the Universe's fundamental energy pattern while he was still in his teens, described his project of creating the structure of all elements using the double-torus concept (*http://www.thrivemovement.com/home*). As we look at all structures in nature, we see elements of the torus in everything. The motion with the torus follows the Fibonacci spiral. That spiral is seen throughout nature, from the snail shells and pine cones, to how a human being is structured in segments following the spiral pattern. (The works of Walter Russell, Nassim Haramein, and Foster Gamble were presented in more detail in Chapter 4, "As Above, So Below — The Formation of Matter.")

On a similar line of thinking, I appreciated the teachings of Arthur Young, which are based on movement in the torus structure. Arthur Young created the Theory of Process, which describes how evolution of the universe occurs. He asked the question, "If the Universe is a machine, and operates according to discoverable rules, what are the rules and, more importantly, what is the purpose of the Universe?" He postulated that the purpose of the universe was to know itself, which would require life and consciousness and the ability to ask the question, "Why?"

Then he used his inventor's hat to declare, "If I was going to invent such a universe, what are the rules that must be followed to allow such a universe to *fly*?" Since he had a wealth of scientific facts by which to test his "invention," he began his quest to discover the rules of the Universe. The results are revealed in the books *The Reflexive Universe: Evolution of Consciousness* and *The Geometry of Meaning*. Dr. Michael Buchele and Bob Whitehouse gave an excellent lecture and workshop on this subject at FMBR in 2011.

BioGeometry was the next major step on my spiritual journey. (BioGeometry was explored in detail in Chapter 9, "Harmony and BioGeometry.") BioGeometry provided me with a new way to look at how the universe is structured, and a way to measure and detect the qualities of harmony through resonance. Dr. Ibrahim Karim rediscovered the ancient understanding and technology of the Egyptians and created the new physics of BioGeometry.

When he went to France on a work assignment from Egypt, he was told to visit the Maison de la Radiesthesia. The older lady at the Maison, who did not know Ibrahim, asked if he was an Egyptian. He said "yes," and the lady said she had been waiting for him. She gave him a treasure trove of notes, books, and instruments from the Maison. Over the years, he discovered the key qualities of harmony through resonance with qualities at sacred power spots.

Resonance with three qualities were present at these power spots. The three qualities together are called BG3, for "BioGeometry 3." The harmonious qualities are a key element in creating the environment for healing. Ibrahim showed that BG3 could harmonize detrimental microwave electromagnetic fields (EMF).

When the new cell towers in Hemberg, Switzerland, disrupted the entire village and caused a significant effect on both humans and animals/birds, Ibrahim's structures — which resonated with BG3 — eliminated the disruptive effects of EMF. Similarly, in a national hepatitis clinical trial, BioGeometry tools (BioSignatures to resonate with the liver) gave results superior to any key drugs for hepatitis. Ibrahim's story is told in *Back to a Future for Mankind: BioGeometry*.

Robert Gilbert from the Vesica Institute gave a fascinating lecture at FMBR on BioGeometry. He was the first instructor for the new field of BioGeometry. After the lecture, I studied Robert's books on the subject.

Ibrahim Karim came and gave another lecture on BioGeometry several years afterwards. FMBR and I were happy to host him. We invited him to our house. However, my wife Peggy could not attend his lecture and had to stay home, since she was having a migraine. When Ibrahim walked into our house, he took a quick look around and figured out some key problems with the EMF at our home and promptly fixed them. He then drew some BioSignatures on Peggy's arm for the migraine, which resulted in a rapid improvement for her.

After a few years, Robert Gilbert came back to the Bay Area, at FMBR's invitation, and taught the Foundation Course in BioGeometry. The course truly explains a lot about how creating harmony works in the human system and in the environment. We learned how to measure the qualities through resonance, and also the fundamentals of radiesthesia.

Using that technique, I can go into any grocery store and test which foods are good for me and which ones I should avoid (i.e., they are not in harmony with me). I can balance a house or a room that may have problems ranging from EMFs to Earth grid lines, and correct the house for the non-harmonious elements.

A few years later, Robert came back and taught the Advanced Course for BioGeometry. Now we could test — with the Archetypal Ruler — problems ranging from the physical plane to problems in the vital, emotional, mental, or spiritual planes and find corrections for those issues. In addition, we learned how to balance the two hemispheres of the brain and to activate its various centers.

An example would be to activate the auditory center. When that happens, you can be in a room with a lot of noise; and after activation, the noise is in harmony and there is a sense of quiet in the midst of the noise. For me, on my journey of seeking, BioGeometry offered me a deeper understanding of the nature of who we are and the subtle energies with which we interact. BioGeometry also taught me some key fundamentals about the role of harmony in healing.

Kriya Yoga

After reading the Indian saint Paramahansa Yogananda's *Autobiography of a Yogi*, I was determined to learn about Kriya Yoga. On the path to learn about oneself, Yogananda convinced me that Kriya Yoga was a key step to clearing karma and making advances in this lifetime. I went to the Ananda Temple (based on Yogananda's teachings) in Palo Alto, California, and learned that you could not just walk in and be taught Kriya Yoga. You would have to take a year-long series of courses and practice in meditation before you would be eligible to learn Kriya. The instructor also had to confirm that you were ready for initiation into Kriya Yoga.

Thus, I signed up for the meditation practices and lectures and went through the course work. The beginning meditation teaches that one is really spirit, and not the body. The real work was the intensive two months at the end of the year where two hours per day of meditation were required, using advanced meditation techniques. The net result of the intensive meditation practices was that at the end of that time, I was able to "hear" the music from all the chakras.

In the Ananda Temple, there is a five-pointed star on a blue background. I had thought it was a symbol/logo for the Temple. However, after the two months' intensive, my third eye was sufficiently opened that I could see the star and the light from the pineal gland. I was thus approved to learn the last step, and was initiated into the practice of Kriya Yoga. Practice of the meditation would allow a person to continue on the spiritual journey. I now understood why the Temple required a full year of practice before teaching the Kriya Yoga.

The World of Spirits and Beyond

The next step on my journey was to learn about the world beyond the current physical matter — the world of spirits and beyond. FMBR invited Luis Minero of the International Academy of Consciousness (IAC) to tell us how to achieve OBE travels (out-of-body-experience). I took the multi-weeks course to learn the fundamentals of OBE. The course was fascinating; I learned multiple techniques, and the classes were quite interesting. I practiced diligently for a year and also tried out the hemi-sync technique of the Monroe Institute. I approached "take-off" many times while in the hypnogogic state, but could never truly take off, though I probably imagined I did several times.

However, I really enjoyed Robert Monroe's books about his OBE adventures, *Journeys Out of the Body*, *Far Journey*, and especially *Ultimate Journey*. These brought him to the higher levels of the spirit world. What I learned from the people who often have OBEs and from reading extensively in this area is that it seems we can travel to other realms while we sleep. I did practice lucid dreaming after listening to Robert Waggoner and reading his book, *Lucid Dreaming: Gateway to the Inner Self*.

Channelings from the Challenger *Crew*

My next journeys would be into the realm of channeling. When Edie Fischer retired from her role as chairman of FMBR, she handed over to me many notes from FMBR's past. Being busy with work, I never looked at the boxes of notes; they sat on my shelf for several years. One day, Edie, along with Bill Gough, mentioned to me that there were some old notes from a channeling that was done 30 years before.

The *Challenger* space shuttle had exploded in 1986, and Jeanne Love and Regina Ochoa had channeled the deceased astronauts. Jeanne, then living in Michigan, was visited in her home by Christa McAuliffe in the evening of the fiery explosion of the *Challenger*. Christa was the first schoolteacher-astronaut; she was hysterical and did not understand what had happened to her. Jeanne, a wonderful channeler, was experiencing Christa's hysteria. All the astronauts were present in Jeanne's home that evening.

Based on Edie's brief introduction, I started reading transcripts of the channelings, which lasted over a period of two years. There was one clear message that all seven astronauts wanted to be delivered: "There is no 'death' and there is 'life' after death." They watched the mourning of their deaths by their families, and really wanted people to know there is no death. They had never realized this important point while they were living.

In order to prove that the channelings were real, there would need to be evidential data. Jeanne's husband was a physicist, and he knew Bob Shacklett, the husband of Edie Fischer and another physicist who belonged to the Foundation for Mind-Being Research (FMBR), which at that time was newly formed. He contacted Bob to see if he could help. Bob, Edie Fischer, and Bill Gough decided to look into this new area of channeling.

The FMBR team would investigate the channeling with the astronauts for the next two years. Jeanne's good friend, and fellow phenomenal channeler, was Regina Ochoa. Both channelers were involved in the many discussions with the astronauts. There were times when both Jeanne and Regina would channel simultaneously, so one astronaut would come in through Jeanne and the other through Regina and two-way conversations could occur among the deceased astronauts. The FMBR team was involved in a number of these channelings and asked the astronauts various pertinent questions.

After reading the transcripts, I wanted to honor the request by the astronauts to get out the message that there is life after death. Over 35 years ago, FMBR tried to get the story written into a book. They had enlisted the help of author John Fuller, who had written *The Airmen Who Would Not Die*. He accepted the project, but he died unexpectedly before he could write the book.

More recently, I spoke with another author who was familiar with channeling. He initially said that he would work on the project, but subsequently decided against it because of other priorities. I thus made the decision that we should just get the transcripts out on the web. I digitalized the three books of typewritten text and organized them by astronaut, and sequentially by time. Several FMBR members volunteered to edit the material I digitalized; our FMBR webmaster put together the website, *https://Challengercc.org/*.

Contact with Jeanne Love and Regina Ochoa had not been made for over 30 years. I needed to get their permission to put the information on the web, but we had no information as to where they lived or how to otherwise contact them. After a little bit of detective work, I found some information on Jeanne and contacted her, and she put me in contact with Regina.

After reading the material that we were planning to make public, Jeanne and Regina thought it over and were okay with putting out the information. It turned out that their initial reluctance in getting into the public eye was that 35 years ago, the government "psyops" had attacked both of them for having channeled the *Challenger* astronauts. ("Psyops" refers to psychic operatives. All key governments have their core of such persons, unknown to the public. Read the transcripts and listen to the recordings of the *Challenger* and *Columbia* astronauts, and you will learn about the one astronaut on every mission who was trained in psychic techniques.) The psyops were able to cause personal harm, and even had one of the channelers shot at with a firearm. The transcripts reveal some sensitive information, which may have contributed to those attacks.

After the website was published, I was conversing with Regina in the car on our way to a Robert Gilbert workshop. Regina suddenly said, "Commander Richard Scobee is here and wants to speak with you." Scobee was the deceased Commander of the *Challenger* Space Shuttle. He asked if I would like to get involved with something big. I did not hesitate — I said, "Definitely!"

Commander Scobee said I would need to form a team, and that he would get back to me. He then said Ellison Onizuka (one of the *Challenger* astronauts) would be with me that day. He also said that when I see Rick Skalsky, to put my hand on his back and some energy would be downloaded to him. Rick and I had started working on research projects involving water, and I knew he would be at Robert Gilbert's workshop. At the workshop, I put my hand on Rick's back and energy was transferred. Rick would be in contact with one of the other astronauts that day.

This would be the beginning of a wonderful relationship with multiple spirits from the other side, working with Jeanne and Regina and our newly formed team. Our many adventures may be relayed in some future writings.

In February, 2019, Jeanne and Regina received a message that the *Columbia* Space Shuttle astronauts, who had died in 2003, wanted to meet with them and our team. None of us knew the purpose of the meeting, but we all gathered to see what would happen. It turned out that the *Columbia* crew, in order not to be burdened with the karma of a fiery death in a future lifetime, needed to re-experience their death to work through problems associated with it.

It was an amazing channeling session, where the astronauts described their transition to the other side. Each had vastly different experiences. The description of them moving over the astral moat, which is filled with the disharmony that Earth has been experiencing, was fascinating.

One of the astronauts, David Brown, was able to view some of the parallel lives he was living in parallel universes based on different decisions. Another astronaut, Kalpana Chawla, was able to experience the joyous reunion with deceased relatives upon returning to an environment resembling her home in India. All of this is described on the FMBR website (*www.FMBR.org*) with links to the *https://challengercc.org/* website, which gives the actual audio recording of communications with *Columbia* astronauts.

I gave myself the task of transcribing the *Columbia* astronauts' recording. As I was transcribing the message from astronaut Sally Ride, she and the other astronauts decided to give me a direct taste of channeling. I was listening to the audio recording of Jeanne channeling Sally when suddenly it was another voice speaking instead of Jeanne. I assumed this was Sally Ride. This was astonishing, since I had never experienced channeling before! I shut off the recorder, but Sally's voice continued a few more minutes with the recorder off. A few months later, *Columbia* astronaut Laurel Clark channeled a message to Regina Ochoa explaining that she and astronaut Judy Resnik had wanted me to experience channeling, and thus had Sally give me that experience.

Where I Am Now

At this stage in my journey, my desire is to help people grow in their consciousness. Everyone is a Divine Being and a Thought Creation of God and thus One with God. For true happiness, people must know that they are the I AM and a co-creator. Understanding the nature of Love, Harmony, and Balance are key.

Since thinking is based on Western science, it would be good to have people exposed to other types of information that reflect on the nature of who we truly are. The information described thus far is meant to help people look at everything in a different light.

I am inherently a researcher, and my goal has been to find evidence/data so that people can know they are much more than they realize. Unfortunately, just talking about their being more than they think they are is too unbelievable for most to consider.

Work with Water

I started working on water with my friend Rick Skalsky. We figured that if we could change water with intention or with our subtle-energy tools, and could measure that change in a reproducible manner, it would offer concrete evidence of who we truly are. We were able to measure changes in the ultraviolet spectrum of water.

The problem was the nature of changes in the control water. Water that was simply in our house/lab would change because of the amount of energies in our homes. For example, I made some distilled water, placed it in a flask, and tested it for the level of BG3. Within a few weeks, the BG3 level had increased considerably. Controls became a difficult problem, as the spectrum would change from week to week.

The experiments with water led me to the work of Marcel Vogel, an IBM scientist who learned to charge and discharge specially structured quartz crystals (Vogel Crystals). These crystals were able to change the structure of water. Marcel employed the crystals for healing and learned some key lessons on the nature of healing. (These were described earlier in Chapter 10: Healing — Harmony and the Self (I AM).")

My research includes concentrating on the 3-6-9 subtle-energy quality. Intuition, divine guidance, and synchronicity led to the discovery of this new "creation" energy. I knew of the sequence 3-6-9 from the work of Nikola Tesla, who said: "If you only knew the magnificence of the 3, 6 and 9, then you would have the key to the universe." The research has expanded to the study of monatomic elements and basics of matter, as seen in the new fields of GANS (Gas in Nano State). The research offers some deep insights in the nature of matter and subtle energies.

Bob Whitehouse came to give a lecture at FMBR in which he showed a cross-section of a torus. In that cross-section, I saw the 3-6-9. I went home and drew the torus. Knowing BioGeometry, I decided to test for BG3. From my work with Walter Russell, I knew that energies go clockwise for creation and counterclockwise for de-creation. I traced the torus structure with clockwise directions and discovered that there now were BG3 energies coming from the structure.

From BioGeometry, I knew that the universe looks at units. Thus, I drew 3-6-9 as units—

||| |||||| |||||||||

—and found BG3. My friend Joachim Wippich had another non-BG3 pendulum, and decided to add the III IIIIII IIIIIIIII markings to the pendulum. That pendulum became good at detecting the BG3 of my drawings. I then tried all the key symbols of creation (Yin Yang symbol, AUM in Sanskrit, Bagua, Marko Rodin's Symbol of Enlightenment) — they all had BG3.

However, when I decided to put in the 3-6-9 symbols onto an emitter sheet (which BioGeometry uses to send BG3 quality to persons needing remote healing), to my surprise the emitter no longer gave off BG3. Thus, I learned that BG3 and 3-6-9 were different qualities. A pendulum with III IIIIII IIIIIIIII etched on it gains the ability to detect/resonate with the 3-6-9 energies.

As Walter Russell's work made clear, God acts as the fulcrum from the middle. That middle is the center of the torus. In carefully measuring it, I found that the torus center does not have BG3, but the whole structure does have BG3. However, the center exhibited resonance with the pendulum that was etched with the 3-6-9 symbols. Thus, I knew that I now had a mechanism to measure the 3-6-9 subtle-energy quality.

It turned out that all the centers of torus, Yin Yang, Bagua, and the Symbol of Enlightenment did not have BG3 in the center, but had 3-6-9 there. Since we are Divine Beings, I measured our central column (our main energy column, where energies of all our chakras are centered). Our general body resonates with BG3. However, our central column does not have BG3, but it does have 3-6-9.

Joachim Wippich now often uses 3-6-9 in his healings since it helps bring people into harmony and the I AM level. My channeling friends call 3-6-9 "the Creation Code," and reported back to me that Nikola Tesla says I am basically correct on my assumptions on the origin of 3-6-9.

Summary and Conclusion

My purpose in telling my story is to put forth a general roadmap of a person with a background as a scientist going through a Seeker's Journey and coming to the same conclusion as the Teacher of Light. Our true essence is I AM; and to find Happiness, Love, and Health, point your compass to achieving Harmony and Balance. My hope is that other Seekers, with the combined stories of Joachim and myself, can be helped in their journey to find their true I AM identity and in achieving Harmony and Balance.

CHAPTER 13

The Mystery of 3-6-9

*"If you only knew the magnificence of the 3, 6 and 9,
then you would have the key to the universe."*
— *Nikola Tesla*

Previous chapters have discussed the nature of spiraling light in the torus structure for the creation of matter; the essence of who we are—I AM; the importance of harmony and balance for our well-being and healing; and the Oneness of everything. We learned that the centering quality of BG3 results in harmony.

In this chapter, these concepts are pulled together in discovering the solution to the mystery of the numbers 3-6-9.

3-6-9: The Key to the Universe

Nikola Tesla (the inventor, engineer, and physicist who invented Alternating Current [AC] generation and transmission technology) used 3-6-9 to help bring in the creative energies in many of his amazing inventions, and went so far as to claim that understanding 3-6-9 would help us to understand the entire universe. His actual words were: "If you only knew the magnificence of the 3, 6 and 9, then you would have the key to the universe."

Through synchronicity and, perhaps, divine download, I instantaneously recognized the answer to Nikola Tesla's statement. I already knew of his statement, since I have been studying his work and life for the past few years. I have also been interacting with Tesla through channeling sessions and experiments, working with channeling mediums Regina Ochoa and Jeanne Love and some friends.

On Oct 25, 2019, when Bob Whitehouse showed a cross-section of the torus at his Foundation for Mind-Body Research lecture, "Divine Design—the Unfolding Torus: Humankind at the Turn with Reason to Hope," I saw the elements of 3, 6, and 9. I then knew that 3-6-9 had to do with the structure of the torus. From my years of research into the nature of who we are and the nature of creation, I knew the importance of the torus structure.

In previous chapters, the basis of matter creation was described as light spiraling centripetally inward to form matter, with the outward spiral resulting in the disintegration of matter. (Recall the discussions on Walter Russell, Nassim Haramein, and Foster Gamble from Chapter 4, "As Above, So Below—The Formation of Matter.") The inward and outward spiraling lights describes the *torus*. The center of the torus is the location of the fulcrum from which the opposing spiraling lights reach balance. All matter is of this construction. Walter Russell also says that our mind (consciousness) is based on this concept. Thus, everything is of this pattern, and we are created in this pattern. This is obviously a simplification of who we are, although the fundamentals remain the same.

Another way to say this is that we are all One and a part of God. We are not separate from God. We are all part of the ocean that is God. The direct knowing of this concept is the basis of enlightenment and of I AM.

Since the torus is fundamental, then the nature of the torus should have some special properties. This chapter will show that the various key symbols and structures that humanity has used in both religions and ancient teachings are in resonance with BG3, the subtle energies of harmony. These subtle energies can be measured. In the process of discovering the nature of the energies of creation and the torus, a new energy of harmony and centering was discovered. It is this that I have named 3-6-9.

Key Religious and Ancient Spiritual Symbols and Structures Resonate with BG3

Both BG3 and 3-6-9 energy qualities are measurable. Anyone can measure them. The act of measuring the resonant-energy qualities, and knowing that they are the symbols described in religions and ancient teachings, provides a sense of knowingness as to the validity of the concepts presented in this chapter. We will describe the following structures, which have both BG3 and 3-6-9 resonant-energetic qualities:

- The numbers 3-6-9 and the Torus
- The Yin Yang Symbol
- AUM in Sanskrit
- The Math of the Torus
- Bagua
- Reiki Symbol of Power

The following sections will describe how to draw some of the structures or symbols to actually *generate* BG3 and 3-6-9 qualities. These structures/symbols have the resonant-energy qualities within them. I shall also teach you how to *detect* the 3-6-9 energy quality. The pendulum tools for detecting and measuring BG3 are available from various distributors associated with BioGeometry.

The Importance and Use of BG3 and 3-6-9 Resonant-Energy Qualities from Structures/Symbols

The importance of these structures/symbols, as well as knowing how to draw them, has to do with *the energy they contain*. Both BG3 and 3-6-9 qualities are inherent in the structures/symbols. Having them in the environment or on the body brings in harmony and centering, just like any BioGeometry tool. The 3-6-9 also has a significant impact on affirmations when they are repeated 3 times, then 6 times, and then 9 times.

Often if I am working with a person for healing purposes, I will draw one of the structures or symbols on a sticker, with the correct direction of rotation (as will be described below), and place the sticker on the person to give them BG3 and 3-6-9 energy qualities. Nikola Tesla also used the symbols to connect to the knowingness of the center to bring him intuition for his many amazing inventions.

The Numbers 3-6-9 and the Torus

After seeing the cross-section of the torus at Bob Whitehouse's lecture and recognizing 3-6-9 within the structure, I went home and drew the torus (see Figure 23, below). In the middle torus, you see the elements of 3-6-9, which I recognized during the lecture. Knowing BioGeometry, I tested the cross-section on the left for BG3, and found none. However, I knew from my work with Walter Russell's discoveries that energies go clockwise for creation (i.e., that creation is based on the centripetal spiral clockwise [CW] direction of light) and counterclockwise for de-creation (i.e., that de-creation is based on the centrifugal spiral counterclockwise [CCW] direction of light). (For a description of BG3 and clockwise rotation whenever BG3 is present, *see* Chapter 9 on "BioGeometry and Harmony.") Consequently, I redrew the cross-section of the torus with the "6" and "9" having clockwise rotation, as seen on the middle torus, below.

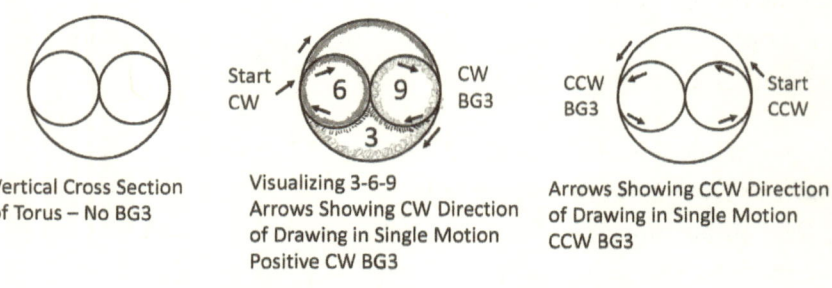

Vertical Cross Section of Torus – No BG3

Visualizing 3-6-9 Arrows Showing CW Direction of Drawing in Single Motion Positive CW BG3

Arrows Showing CCW Direction of Drawing in Single Motion CCW BG3

Drawing direction of energy flow or just putting arrows for direction creates BG3

FIGURE 23. Visualizing 3-6-9 in Torus / BG3 within Torus

Instruction on Drawing the Torus to Show BG3

Look at the cross-section of the middle torus structure that has the numbers 3, 6, and 9. There is an arrow with the words "Start CW." Using a pen or pencil, as the arrow indicates, start tracing the smaller circle that says "6" in a clockwise (CW) manner. After completing the tracing of the circle containing the "6," continue tracing the larger circle in a clockwise manner. At the middle of the edge of the smaller circle with number "9," you can see that you have traced the number "6."

Now, upon reaching the edge of the smaller circle that says "9," start tracing the smaller circle from the middle in a clockwise manner, as indicated by the arrows. When you reach the starting point of the smaller circle labeled "9," continue tracing the larger circle downward until you reach the middle of the circle labeled "6." You have now completed tracing the number "9."

You can also see the number "3" that is formed by the two smaller circles. The entire pattern is drawn in one continuous motion, without reversing directions. When the torus structure is drawn in this manner, the torus emits BG3, which can be measured with the BG3 pendulum (a clockwise rotation of the pendulum).

It is interesting to note that by merely putting arrows on a torus to show the direction of energy flow, the torus generates BG3. Tracing energy flow on the torus without arrows or just drawing the torus as described above results in BG3. In photocopying a torus showing BG3, the photocopy, too, will have BG3.

A note about the negative counterclockwise BG3: Although I show the directions of arrows to draw a torus with CCW rotation, I am not giving detailed instructions on drawing it, since it is not an emitter of positive BG3 or 3-6-9 energies. It is simply shown for completeness of information sharing.

The Numbers 3-6-9

We saw how the numbers 3-6-9 were embedded in the torus structure—i.e., the numbers themselves are part of the torus. If one writes the numbers "3-6-9," there is no BG3. However, if the numbers 6 and 9 are written with a CW direction, as indicated by the arrows in the figure below, there *are* BG3 and 3-6-9 energies (to be described later in this chapter). Similarly, if the direction is CCW, there is CCW rotation of the BG3 pendulum. A mix of CW and CCW rotation for the 6 and 9

THE SEEKER AND THE TEACHER OF LIGHT

does not show BG3; and if the 3 is drawn in reverse with CW 6 and 9, there is no BG3.

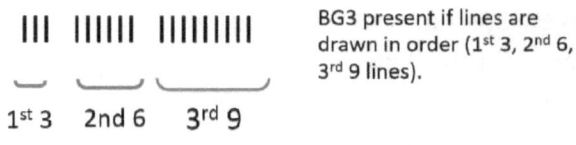

3 6 9	3 6 9	3 6 9	3 6 9
Positive BG3 Rotation 6 & 9 CW	Negative BG3 Rotation 6 & 9 CCW	No BG3 No Rotation 6 CCW 9 CW	No BG3 No Rotation 3 Reverse, 6 & 9 CW

FIGURE 24. The numbers 3-6-9 and BG3

In BioGeometry, we learn that the universe looks at units when talking about numbers. Thus, one can write 3-6-9 as seen in Figure 25, below.

III IIIIII IIIIIIIII	BG3 present if lines are drawn in order (1st 3, 2nd 6, 3rd 9 lines).
1st 3 2nd 6 3rd 9	

FIGURE 25. 3-6-9 as vertical units

Writing 3-6-9 as lines or dots results in BG3. When working on a person for healing, it is often very easy to write III IIIIII IIIIIIIII on a sticker to bring in harmony.

Creating and Using a 3-6-9 Pendulum

Using the principles of resonance, you can easily make a pendulum for detecting the resonant-energy qualities of 3-6-9. Simply putting 3 lines, then 6 lines, and 9 lines onto a pendulum—with a space between the 3 groups of lines—will convert the pendulum into a 3-6-9 pendulum, which then can detect the 3-6-9 energies by resonance. When 3-6-9 energy qualities are detected, the pendulum will rotate in a clockwise rotation. Just hold the pendulum above a source of 3-6-9 energies, start the to-and-fro movement, and the pendulum will rotate clockwise above the 3-6-9 energy source.

To put the 3-6-9 lines onto a pendulum, you can use a fine Sharpie pen to draw the lines. Alternatively, on a harder surface such as a metal or ceramic pendulum, you can write (etch/scratch) the lines with an inexpensive carbide pen (get the least expensive one—I bought mine for less than $10). Then simply write the 3, 6, and 9 lines on the pendulum. (You can refer back to the recipe in Chapter 8 for making an inexpensive pendulum out of salt and flour, or any polymer clay from a craft store.) To make the pendulum an even stronger resonator of 3-6-9 energies, you can write two or more sets of 3, 6, 9 lines on different places on the pendulum.

As you learn to draw structures/symbols with 3-6-9 energies for healing and harmony applications, the pendulum works to detect the resonant-energy qualities, which will tell you whether you drew the symbol or lines correctly. Incidentally, most items that give off BG3 energy qualities also give off 3-6-9 energy qualities, so a 3-6-9 pendulum can detect the energies if both are present. Later in the chapter, I will describe why 3-6-9 and BG3 energies are not identical.

Notes on the Use of 3-6-9 and BG3 Pendulums

The use of the 3-6-9 pendulum is the same as in the fields of radiesthesia and BioGeometry. Those who practice radiesthesia or BioGeometry will have no problem detecting 3-6-9. For detecting BG3, see the pendulums from BioGeometry (e.g., BG16 or IKUP pendulums). They are available from various BioGeometry distributors (e.g., *www.FMBR.org*).

To learn how to use a pendulum based on radiesthesia principles, see Robert Gilbert's *The Neutral Pendulum* on YouTube (*https://youtu.be/rklULOn8p0w*).

In radiesthesia, once you have initiated the motion of the pendulum, the pendulum will rotate clockwise when you come into resonance with the 3-6-9 subtle energy. Similarly, with a BG3 pendulum, the pendulum will rotate clockwise when BG3 is present. When 3-6-9 is present, the 3-6-9 pendulum will rotate clockwise.

The Yin Yang Symbol

The purpose of the yin yang symbol/structure is to demonstrate that there is polarity (male/female) in everything, and that when things are in balance there is harmony. This is reminiscent of the male (red)-female (blue) spiraling light from Walter Russell's description of cosmology (*see* Chapter 4, "As Above, So Below—The Formation of Matter").

In investigating 3-6-9, I was led to look at the yin yang symbol (see the illustration at left in the graphic below). I checked to see whether it had BG3, and no BG3 was detected. However, I found that if the yin yang symbol is drawn with a single motion (as shown in the center illustration), BG3 is present. If one continues the drawing in a single motion (illustration at right), the cross-section of the torus is created, which has BG3. Thus, it is not surprising that there is BG3, since the yin yang symbol is part of the torus structure.

YIN YANG IS PART OF THE VERTICAL CROSS SECTION OF A TORUS

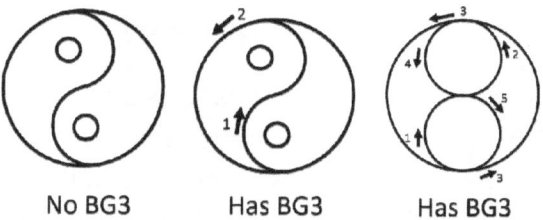

No BG3   Has BG3   Has BG3

FIGURE 26. Yin Yang is part of the vertical cross-section of a torus

Figure 27, below, shows an image of the top view of a torus. You can see the yin yang spiral in it (the darker curved line).

FIGURE 27. Yin Yang spiral in the torus (view from above)

The yin yang structure is unique, since it brings in both CW and CCW motion. This likely represents bringing into harmony the yin (female) and yang (male) aspects. The power of the symbol is to bring in harmony. This is the reason why, in a later section that discusses harmonizing the BG3 and 3-6-9 energies, we can use the yin yang symbol. Because of the harmonizing nature of the symbol, we can also draw the line within the symbol with both CW and CCW directions. In fact, if one starts with a circle, one only needs to draw the spiraling line indicating the elements of yin and yang to generate the BG3 and 3-6-9 aspects of the circle, as shown below in Figure 28.

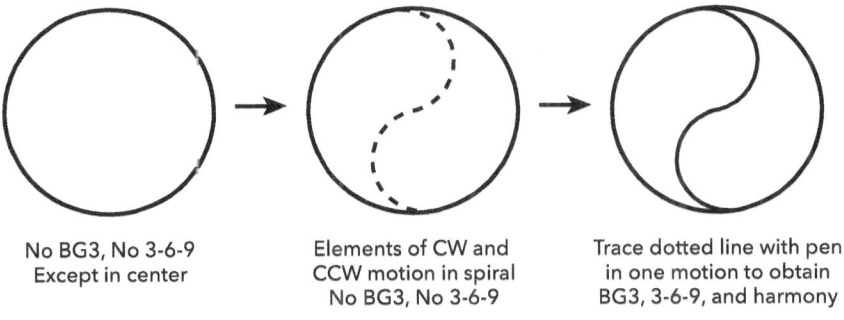

No BG3, No 3-6-9
Except in center

Elements of CW and
CCW motion in spiral
No BG3, No 3-6-9

Trace dotted line with pen
in one motion to obtain
BG3, 3-6-9, and harmony

FIGURE 28. Harmony from joining CW and CCW spiral

AUM in Sanskrit

There are various meanings attributed to AUM. AUM is often used to refer to the cause of the Universe, the essence of life, Brahman (ultimate reality, entirety of the universe, truth, divine, supreme spirit, cosmic principles, knowledge), Atman (Soul, self within), and Self-knowledge. Hindus believe that the mantra "AUM (or "OM)" is the name of God, the vibration of the Supreme. It is sometimes chanted as three sounds—A-U-M, symbolic of the three major Hindu deities: Brahma Shakti (creation); Vishnu Shakti (preservation); and Shiva Shakti (liberation, and/or destruction).

The AUM mantra is composed of four elements: the first three are vocal sounds:

1. A,

2. U, and
3. M.
4. The fourth sound, unheard, is the *silence* that begins and ends the audible sound; the silence that surrounds it.

As creation began, the divine, all-encompassing consciousness took the form of the first and original vibration, manifesting as the sound AUM. It is also suggested that the three phonetic components of *AUM* (*a* + *u* + *m*) correspond to the three stages of cosmic creation, and that—when read or said—AUM celebrates the creative powers of the universe. Some say to chant AUM three times, since it symbolizes the three worlds of the Soul: the past, the present and the future.

Nkunj Bangad, in a blog about "Why did Tesla say that 3-6-9 was the key to the universe?" wrote that AUM is related to 3-6-9. I looked up AUM in the various languages of the world and found that only the Sanskrit version of AUM had BG3.

Below in Figure 29 is the correlation of AUM with 3-6-9. Since the AUM, written in Sanskrit, is part of the torus structure of creation, it is not surprising to find that the symbol has both BG3 and 3-6-9 energies.

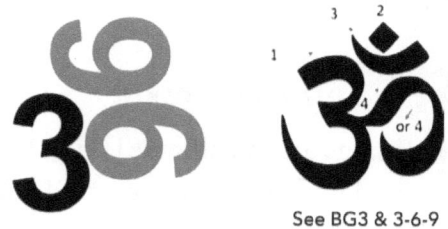

See BG3 & 3-6-9

FIGURE 29. 3-6-9 and AUM

The Math of the Torus

Randy Powell, taking the sequence of numbers from the Vortex Math structure of Marko Rodin, discovered that the math extrapolates to the structure of the torus. Marko Rodin discovered that in the sequence of numbers, the numbers 3, 6, 9 were unique. The number 9 was the king of numbers (e.g., if you multiply any number with 9, the digital root remains 9: e.g., 9 x 3 = 27 and its digital root is 2 +7 = 9). The numbers

The Mystery of 3-6-9

3 and 6 seem to "vibrate" with themselves or with 9 (e.g., 2 x 3 = 6; 6 x 5 = 30 and its digital root is 3 + 0 = 3). All the other numbers form a sequence of 1 — 2 — 4 — 8 — 7 — 5 — 1 (e.g., if you double 1 you get the next number, which is 2; if you double 8 you get 16 (with the digital root being 1 + 6 = 7). One could postulate that the "material world" could be represented by 1 — 2 — 4 — 8 — 7 — 5 — 1, with 3, 6, 9 being the separate trinity. Thus, the Vortex Math structure is sometimes called the Symbol of Enlightenment. This makes more sense when you consider the torus as being the basis of creation. The Vortex Math structure is shown shown in Figure 30, below:

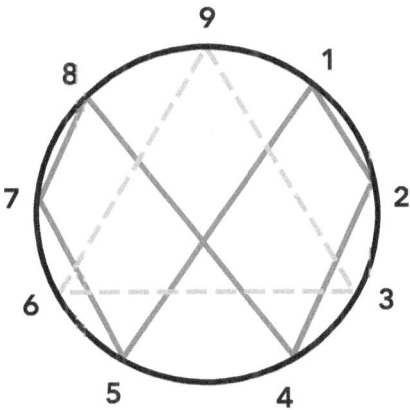

FIGURE 30. The Vortex Math structure

The structure itself does not show the energy qualities of BG3, nor 3-6-9. However, if you trace the lines linking 1 — 2 — 4 — 8 — 7 — 5 — 1 in sequence, you do get BG3 and 3-6-9 energy qualities. This structure is shown below, with arrows showing the sequence of connecting the numbers. Based on the BioGeometry principle that the universe sees numbers as units, if one writes the sequence as lines, the sequence of lines generates BG3 and 3-6-9 energy qualities. Thus, if, in a healing session, one wants to bring in the harmony of 3-6-9, one can draw

| || |||| |||||||| |||||||| ||||| |

on a sticker and give it to the person to generate greater harmony and centering.

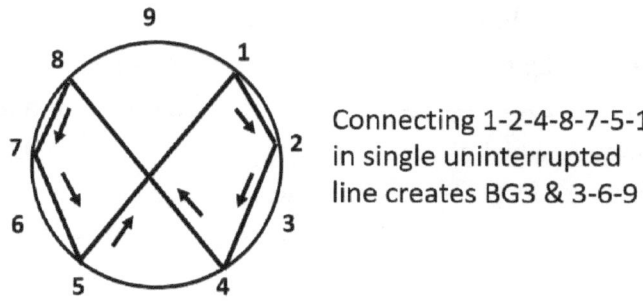

FIGURE 31. The Vortex Math Structure with connecting lines, producing 3-6-9 and BG3

Bagua

The Bagua or Pa Kua are eight symbols used in Taoist cosmology to represent the fundamental principles of reality, seen as a range of eight interrelated concepts. Each consists of three lines, each line either "broken" or "unbroken," respectively representing yin or yang. Due to their tripartite structure, they are often referred to as Eight Trigrams in English.

The trigrams are related to Taiji philosophy, Taijiquan, and the Wu Xing, or "five elements." The relationships between the trigrams are represented in two arrangements: (1) the *Primordial* "Earlier Heaven," or "Fu Xi" bagua, and (2) the *Manifested* "Later Heaven," or "King Wen" bagua. The trigrams have correspondences in astronomy, astrology, geography, geomancy, anatomy, the family, and elsewhere.

The ancient Chinese classic *I Ching* (Pinyin: Yi Jing) consists of the 64 pairwise permutations of trigrams, referred to as "hexagrams," along with commentary on each one.

The connection of the bagua structure to the torus comes from the work of Nassim Haramein, in which he links the 64 tetrahedrons of the isotropic vector matrix to the formation of the double torus. This may link to the 64 trigrams of the I Ching, which is derived from the bagua.

The bagua structure, shown in Figure 32, below, similarly has BG3 and 3-6-9 energetic resonance qualities.

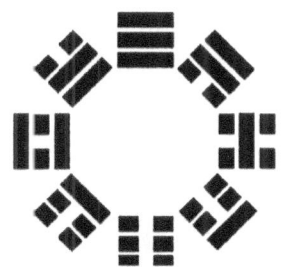

FIGURE 32. The Bagua structure

Reiki Symbol of Power

Reiki is a spiritual healing art of Japanese origin. The word *Reiki* comes from the Japanese word (Rei), which means "Universal Life," and (Ki), which means "Energy." Reiki is not affiliated with any particular religion or religious practice. Dr. Mikao Usui, a Japanese Buddhist monk, brought the healing practice of Reiki into prominence in the mid 1800s. The physical part of Reiki is the use of energy from the hands for the purpose of healing. Dr. Usui taught that the healer's purpose is also to help people realize that healing the spirit by consciously deciding to improve oneself is a necessary part of the Reiki healing experience.

All Symbols have BG3 energy
FIGURE 33. Reiki symbols

Reiki practitioners learn to mentally project Reiki symbols onto the palm of their hand before placing that hand onto the person needing healing. Testing the Reiki symbols with the BG3 pendulum showed that all symbols had BG3 harmonizing-energy qualities, as shown in Figure 33, above.

However, only the power symbol showed both BG3 and 3-6-9 resonant-energy qualities, as shown in Figure 34, below.

FIGURE 34. The Reiki power symbol (has BG3 and 3-6-9)

To me, it appears that the power symbol shows the clockwise spiraling of light energy in the torus structure. There are three spirals representing the number 3. In Chinese and Japanese writing, the direction and order of writing is important. The power symbol has the spiral starting from the center and going in a clockwise direction, resulting in the formation of BG3 and 3-6-9 energy qualities. If one starts drawing the power symbol from the outside, the spiral will be in a counterclockwise direction and there will be no BG3 and 3-6-9.

BG3 Is Different from 3-6-9

It should be noted that BG3 is not the same as 3-6-9; and sometimes, when a BG3 tool is used along with a 3-6-9 symbol/structure, there is negation of both energy qualities. I mention this point because some readers may work with BG3 tools to harmonize an environment or person, and also may want to use a 3-6-9 symbol or structure to augment the levels of harmony. They should realize that, under certain circumstances, both BG3 and 3-6-9 resonant-energy qualities can be nullified. An example follows.

BioGeometry offers a variety of tools to increase the level of BG3 in an environment. As an example, in BioGeometry the L-90 structure is in the shape of an "L," along with part of a circle. BG3 is found within the 90-degree angle formed by the "L." When you put the L-90 together with the 3-6-9 as lines and test for BG3 and 3-6-9 energy qualities, you find that both energy qualities are not present, as shown in Figure 35 (A–C), below.

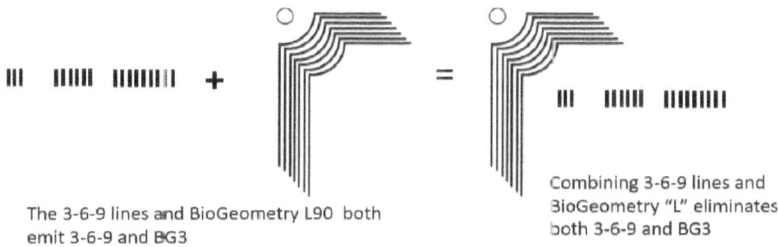

The 3-6-9 lines and BioGeometry L90 both emit 3-6-9 and BG3

Combining 3-6-9 lines and BioGeometry "L" eliminates both 3-6-9 and BG3

FIGURE 35. The L-90 structure and the 3-6-9 lines
(A) Mixing some 3-6-9 and BG3 tools may nullify both qualities

However, by inviting in harmony, the nullifying of BG3 and 3-6-9 is eliminated and both BG3 and 3-6-9 are present. A possible hypothesis as to what is happening is that the vibrations for BG3 and 3-6-9 are different and can interfere and nullify their respective resonant energy qualities. The power of bringing in harmony is significant and brings the interference into harmony. This is shown in Figure 35-B, below.

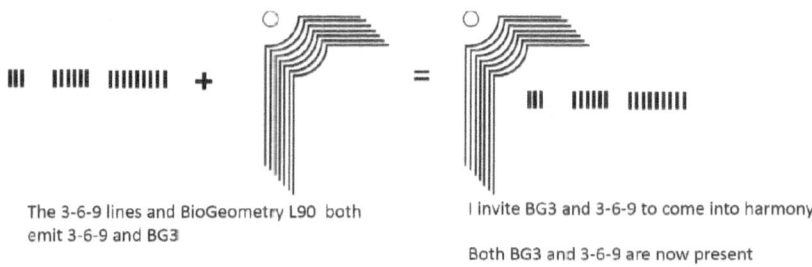

The 3-6-9 lines and BioGeometry L90 both emit 3-6-9 and BG3

I invite BG3 and 3-6-9 to come into harmony

Both BG3 and 3-6-9 are now present

(B) The mixed 3-6-9 and BG3 tools and their energy qualities can be harmonized

The yin yang symbol is known to be the balance of the yin and yang qualities to produce harmony. Thus, introducing the yin yang symbol may bring in harmony when there is a BG3 and a 3-6-9 tool. That was found to be the case, as shown in Figure 35-C, below.

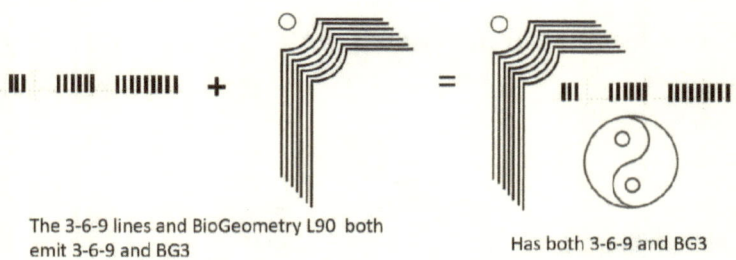

The 3-6-9 lines and BioGeometry L90 both emit 3-6-9 and BG3

Has both 3-6-9 and BG3

(C) Adding yin yang with 3-6-9 and BG3 tools eliminates nullifying effect of both 3-6-9 and BG3 combination

For those people who use BioGeometry items to increase the level of BG3 in an environment and would also like to use a 3-6-9 symbol or structure, it's advisable to test whether there is interference. This testing is done with the BG3-detecting pendulum, which can be purchased from distributors selling BioGeometry items. (The 3-6-9-detecting pendulums and their construction were described in the "Creating and Using a 3-6-9 Pendulum" section of this chapter.) If there is interference, simply say or write, "I invite BG3 and 3-6-9 to come into harmony."

The alternative is to add in a yin yang symbol that has been activated to give BG3 and 3-6-9 by drawing it, as described in the yin yang section in this chapter. From my experience, if the BG3 and 3-6-9 items/structures are separated (e.g., 1 foot apart), there is no interference. However, if items are placed on top of each other or close together, as in the case of the L-90 and 3-6-9 lines, then negative interference can occur.

The implication of the interference with BG3 items and 3-6-9 items indicates that the resonant qualities of BG3 and 3-6-9 are different, even though most items we have discussed have both BG3 and 3-6-9 resonant-energy qualities.

Location of 3-6-9 and BG3 Resonant-Energy Qualities in Torus Structures

I reviewed the 3-6-9 patterns based on the torus structure for the location of BG3 and 3-6-9. Within the torus structure, the center is the "still point" from which everything emanates and everything must pass. (*See* Chapter 4: "As Above, So Below—The Formation of Matter.") The question I had in mind was whether the resonating subtle quality at this still point was different from the subtle quality elsewhere in the structure. The finding was that when the torus structure was drawn in a CW manner, it had BG3; however, the center showed no BG3, but it did have the 3-6-9 energy quality. This is shown in Figure 36, below.

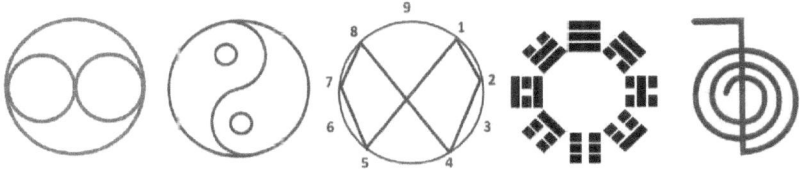

All structures have BG3 and 3-6-9 energy for whole structure

All structures lack BG3 at the center

The centers of all structures have 3-6-9 energy

FIGURE 36. Various torus structures (drawn clockwise) containing BG3 except in the center, which does have 3-6-9

It appears that the *center* of the various 3-6-9 symbols and structures that are torus/circular shaped constitutes the basis of this resonant subtle-energy quality. One might speculate that *the center of a torus is the point of balance from which creation occurs*. Within matter and for galaxies, this might be considered the center of the black hole. (Nassim Haramein states that all atoms are centered with black holes.)

In Walter Russell's terminology, God is at the fulcrum of creation, controlling it but not of it. Perhaps 3-6-9 belongs to the central, controlling aspect of creation—aligned with the I AM. It also appears that 3-6-9 often coincides with the harmony energy of BG3 but is distinct and different from BG3.

It is interesting to note that if one tests for BG3 in the human *being*, one finds BG3 everywhere on the body of the person, except for the central column of the person (the axis through the spinal cord). However, if one tests for 3-6-9 in the human *body*, one finds 3-6-9 everywhere on the body, including the central column of the person. It appears that there is some commonality between finding 3-6-9 in the center of the torus structure and in the center of the human structure.

The Spiritual Aspect of 3-6-9

The nature of 3-6-9 has a spiritual side. The basis of 3-6-9 is creation. All of creation is based on the same concept—the toroidal inward and outward vortex flows. There is also the polar aspect of the two lights (red and blue) forming the toroidal flows. God is at the center, balancing all. However, for created matter, because of polarity, there can be imbalances.

Love, Harmony/Balance is at the center of 3-6-9, the toroidal center. When Love, Harmony/Balance is there, happiness is also there. When there are imbalances or disharmony, there is a seeking of harmony to bring everything back into balance. Love is a primary tool to re-establish Harmony. The conscious invitation to the elements that are out of harmony to come back into harmony is often all that is needed to heal a problem.

Love and Harmony/Balance appear to be integral to 3-6-9. The use of any of the 3-6-9 symbols (e.g., 3 lines, then 6 lines, and then 9 lines) will often create the harmony needed for manifestation of desired loving outcomes. Repeating any of the Harmony affirmations and any of the I AM affirmations 3 times, 6 times, and finally 9 times can bring one to Harmony and to the I AM vibrational frequency.

The Healing Aspect of 3-6-9

As with BG3, the 3-6-9 symbols and structures and pendulum have a harmonizing effect, which is useful for healing work. These symbols and structures can be drawn on stickers and placed on the body for a harmonizing effect.

Joachim and I have used 3-6-9 in a variety of ways. From our BioGeometry teachings, we can point to or visually connect with a person's problem area (pain) with the intent of offering that area BG3 resonant-energy quality. The pendulum will rotate clockwise for a few minutes to allow BG3 to resonate with the problem area.

You can do exactly the same procedure with the 3-6-9 pendulum. You can connect with the problem area and allow clockwise rotation to occur with that area. Clockwise rotation will occur until resonance has been completed.

The power of affirmations is significantly augmented when they are repeated 3 times, then 6 times, and finally 9 times. This technique is very useful for any of the affirmations described in this book. For example, in healing, you can repeat a harmonizing, healing, or I AM affirmation (*see* Chapter 11: "Joachim Wippich—Teacher of Light") 3 times, then 6 times, and finally 9 times, to augment the occurrence of healing. Sometimes repeating an affirmation once is insufficient for the meaning of that affirmation to become a part of the individual's thought patterns. Repeating it 3, 6, and 9 times significantly brings the affirmation to the forefront of a person's thinking.

Summary of Key Points in This Chapter

- A new centering, harmonizing energy quality has been discovered, which is linked to the fundamental structure of creation — the torus.
- The mystery and secret of the 3-6-9 numbers are associated with the torus structure.
- The symbols of creation are associated with the torus structure: AUM, Yin Yang, Bagua, Reiki Power Symbol, Rodin's Symbol of Enlightenment.
- Drawing the symbols of creation and 3-6-9, using the spiraling direction (CW) for creation, manifests the harmonizing resonant-energy quality.
- The harmonizing energy qualities can also be manifested numerically in terms of lines representing 3-6-9

and 1-2-4-8-7-5-2

- A pendulum can be made that resonates with the 3-6-9 energy qualities and thus can detect it. When detected by the 3-6-9 pendulum, the name given to that energy is 3-6-9.
- The symbols and structures have both BG3 and 3-6-9 subtle energy qualities.
- Sometimes, putting BG3-generating items and 3-6-9-generating symbols and structures together results in nullifying both energy qualities.
- The 3-6-9 symbols and structures can be used to produce harmony in the environment and on the person. It is thus useful when working on a person for healing.
- Use of the symbols help to raise the vibrational level of the person wearing/using the symbols (e.g., as a sticker with the drawing of the symbol or lines).
- Repeating affirmations 3 times, 6 times, then 9 times significantly increases the effectiveness of the affirmations.
- From the spiritual side, understanding that creation uses the torus for manifesting all matter from light allows us to know that we are all light and of the One Mind of God.

Conclusion

As a conclusion to this book, let's bring in harmony using the yin yang symbol and bringing yourself to your I AM essence level with a simple affirmation.

At the very start of this book, you generated harmony by drawing over the dotted spiral of the yin yang symbol with a pen or pencil, using one continuous motion. That symbol is reproduced below.

Now that you have read Chapter 13 on 3-6-9 and Chapter 8 on dowsing, you can use your 3-6-9 pendulum (made by putting III IIIII IIIIIIII on a neutral pendulum) and test the yin yang symbol before drawing over the dotted line. The yin yang symbol will not have 3-6-9 energies (there will be no clockwise rotation of the pendulum). Draw over the dotted line with a pen, and the yin yang symbol will be activated and bring in harmony (clockwise motion of pendulum).

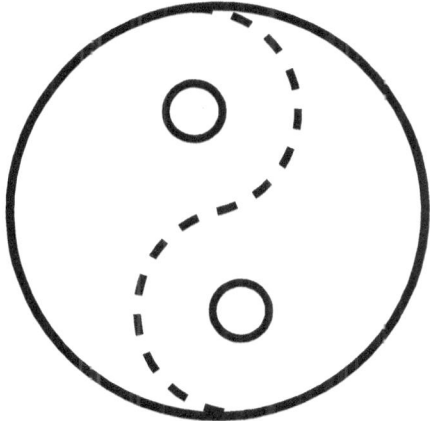

Now bring yourself to the I AM vibrational level by using the simplified I AM affirmation below:

"I AM" (breath), **"I AM"** (breath), **"I AM"** (breath)

State this 3 times with a conscious inhalation of breath on the "I" and a conscious exhalation of breath on the "AM." This allows the I AM meaning/essence to register with you.

"I am rethinking I AM, I AM, I AM, I AM, I AM, I AM"

Repeating "I AM" 6 times.

"I am rethinking I AM, I AM, I AM, I AM, I AM, I AM, I AM, I AM, I AM"

Repeating "I AM" 9 times.

"I AM [Full Birth Name] I AM"

Dowse and check your I AM vibrational level with your pendulum.

References: Text

Chapter 3: You Are Not Just Your Body

Hydrocephalus studies:

Roger Lewin, "Is Your Brain Really Necessary?" *Science* (12 December 1980). 210 (4475): 1232–1234. doi:10.1126/science.7434023. PMID 7434023

_____, "Is Your Brain Really Necessary? Revisited," *Discover* (26 July 2015; retrieved 9 February 2020).

How birds fly:

Peter Friederici, "How a Flock of Birds Can Flock Together," *Audubon Magazine* (March-April 2009).

https://www.audubon.org/magazine/march-april-2009/how-flock-birds-can-fly-and-move-together

The Human Creative Formula:

Caroline Cory, film: "Superhuman: The Invisible Made Visible"

https://www.youtube.com/watch?v=X4rW3Tl3jX8

_____, *The Visible and Invisible Worlds of God*. iUniverse, 2004.

Cleve Backster experiments:

Cleve Backster, *Primary Perception: Biocommunication with Plants, Living Foods, and Human Cells*. White Rose Millennium Press, 2003.

PEAR Labs:

R. D. Nelson, J. M. Bradish, Y. H. Dobyn, B. J. Dunne, and R. G. Jahn, "Field RGE Anomalies in Group Situations," *Journal of Scientific Exploration*, 10:111-42 (1996).

Dean Radin, "Global Consciousness Project Analysis for September 11, 2001," Institute of Noetic Sciences, 2001. *http://noosphere.princeton.edu/dean/wtc0921.html*

R. Jahn and B. C. Dunne, *Consciousness and the Source of Reality*. ICRL Press, 2011.

Double-Slit Experiment:

https://en.wikipedia.org/wiki/Double-slit_experiment#:~:text=In%20 modern%20physics%2C%20the%20double,nature%20of%20quantum%20 mechanical%20phenomena.

Kirlian Photography and more:

https://en.wikipedia.org/wiki/Kirlian_photography#Scientific_research

Konstantin Korotkov, "Gas Discharge Visualization," *https://www.korotkov.eu/*

Chakras:

Master Choa, *The Chakras and their Functions.* Institute for Inner Studies Publishing Foundation, Inc., 2012.

Biogeometry and Radiesthesia:

https://www.biogeometry.ca

https://www.biogeometry.ca/radiesthesia

Remote Viewing:

Russell Targ, "Third Eye Spies" video. Available on Amazon Prime: *https://www.amazon.com/Third-Eye-Spies-Russell-Targ/dp/B07NZ7Z37V* and other online venues. Trailer: *https://www.youtube.com/watch?v=KAT_3CBBOk0*

Healing:

Bill Bengston and Sylvia Fraser, *The Energy Cure: Unraveling the Mystery of Hands-On Healing.* Sounds True, 2010.

Barbara Ann Brennan, *Hands of Light: A Guide to Healing through the Human Energy Field.* Bantam, 1988.

Death Is Just a Journey to Another Level of Vibration:

Near-Death Experiences (NDEs):

Eben Alexander, *Proof of Heaven: A Neurosurgeon's Journey into the Afterlife.* Simon & Schuster, 2012.

Anita Moorjani, *Dying to Be Me: My Journey from Cancer, to Near Death, to True Healing.* Hay House, 2012.

Lynn Vincent and Todd Burpo, *Heaven Is for Real: A Little Boy's Astounding Story of His Trip to Heaven and Back.* Thomas Nelson, 2010 (also a movie).

Out-of-Body Experiences (OBEs):

International Academy of Consciousness: *https://www.iacworld.org/*

Robert A. Monroe, *Journeys Out of the Body.* Broadway Books, 1992 (updated edition).

_____, *Far Journeys.* Harmony, 1987 (reissue edition).

The Monroe Institute: *https://www.monroeinstitute.org/*

Mediums and Channeling:
www.ChallengerCC.org

Dan Drasin, "Calling Earth": *https://vimeo.com/101171248*

Foundation for Body/Mind Research (FMBR): *https://fmbr.org/*

Mark Ireland, *Messages from the Afterlife: A Bereaved Father's Journey in the World of Spirit Visitations, Psychic-Mediums, and Synchronicity*. North Atlantic Books, 2013.

Hypnosis and Regression:
Raymond Moody, *Life after Life*. HarperOne, 2015 (anniversary special edition).

Michael Newton, *Journey of Souls: Case Studies of Life Between Lives*

Chapter 4: As Above, So Below – The Formation of Matter
Walter Russell's View of Creation:
Glenn Clark, *The Man Who Tapped the Secrets of the Universe*. (1946) Univ of Science & Philosophy, 1989.

Walter Russell, *The Secret of Light* (1947). Bridger House Publishers, 2018.

_____, *The Message of the Divine Iliad,* Volumes I and II (1948-1949). Univ of Science & Philosophy, 1971.

_____, *A New Concept of the Universe.* Univ of Science & Philosophy, 1971.

_____, *The Universal One*. Univ of Science & Philosophy, 1977.

A Clairvoyant Understanding of the Atom:
Charles Leadbeater and Annie Besant, *Occult Chemistry: Investigations by Clairvoyant Magnification into the Structure of the Atoms of the Periodic Table and Some Compounds.* (1908) Kessinger Publishing, 2010.

The Torus:
Foster Gamble, *www.thrivemovement.com*

Nassim Haramein, "Crossing the Event Horizon: Rise to the Equation" (DVD)

_____, and Elizabeth A. Rauscher, "Spinors, Twistors, Quaternions, and the 'Spacetime' Torus Topology," *International Journal of Computing Anticipatory Systems,* D. Dubois (ed.), Institute of Mathematics, Liege University, Belgium, ISSN 1373-5411, 2007.

Arthur M. Young, *The Reflexive Universe: Evolution of Consciousness*. Anados Foundation, 1999 (revised edition).

Chapter 5: How We Create from Our Thoughts
Creating a Desired Reality:
Caroline Cory, *The Visible and Invisible Worlds of God*. iUniverse, 2004.

Owen Waters, *Spirituality Made Simple*. Infinite Being, 2019.

Chapter 6: I AM
Cynthia Spring and Frances Vaughan, *Seven Questions About Life After Life: A Collaboration between Two Souls, One Incarnate on Earth and One on the Other Side Who Share a Greater Reality.* Book One in the "Greater Reality" Series. Wisdom Circles Publishing, 2019.

_____, *Seven Questions About the Greater Reality,* Book Two in the "Greater Reality" Series. Wisdom Circles Publishing, 2020.

Chapter 7: Harmony and Balance
Joe Vitale and Ihaleakala Hew Len, *Zero Limits: The Secret Hawaiian System for Wealth, Health, Peace, and More.* Wiley, 2008.

Chapter 8: Vibrational Level and Dowsing
American Society of Dowsers (ASD): *https://dowsers.org/*

BioGeometry Foundation courses: *https://www.biogeometry.ca/courses-events*

Robert Gilbert, YouTube video on the use of the neutral pendulum: *https://youtu.be/rklULOn8p0w*

Vesica Institute: *https://vesica.org, https://vesica.org/bg-courses/*

Walt Woods, *Letter to Robin: A Mini-Course on Pendulum Dowsing.* Walter Woods, 1998 (revised edition).

Chapter 9: Harmony and BioGeometry
A. de Belizal and P.A. Morel, *Physique Micro-Vibratoire et Forces Invisible.* Paris: Desforges, 1976.

www.biogeometry.ca/biogeometry-faq

Leon Chaumery and A. de Belizal, *Essai de Radiesthesie Vibratoire* (4th edition). Paris: Desforges, 1976.

Ibrahim Karim, *Back to a Future for Mankind: BioGeometry.* Createspace, 2010.

_____ *BioGeometry Signatures: Harmonizing the Body's Subtle Energy Exchange with the Environment.* Createspace, 2016.

BioGeometry courses:
BioGeometry Foundation (*https://www.biogeometry.ca/courses-events*).

Vesica Institute (*https://vesica.org/*)

Chapter 10: Healing – Harmony and the Self (I AM)
Marcel Vogel, "The Crystal Wisdom of Marcel Vogel": *https://www.satyacenter.com/crystal-wisdom-of-marcel-vogel*

BioGeometry Foundation Training Notes — on Healing

Chapter 12: Journey of a Seeker

The *Challenger* channeled transcripts: *https://Challengercc.org/*

Caroline Cory, *The Visible & Invisible Worlds of God*. iUniverse, 2004.

_____, *God Among Us: Inside the Mind of the Divine Masters*. OMnium Books, 2005.

_____, *The Divine Plan Beyond 2012*. OMnium Books, 2007.

Eliza Mada Dalian, *In Search of the Miraculous: Healing into Consciousness*. iUniverse 2009.

_____, *Healing the Body & Awakening Consciousness with the Dalian Method: An Advanced Self-Healing System for a New Humanity*. Expanding Universe Publishing, 2014.

FMBR website (*www.FMBR.org*) with links to the *https://challengercc.org/* website, which gives the actual audio recording of communications with *Columbia* astronauts.

Norman Friedman and Fred Alan Wolf, *Bridging Science and Spirit: Common Elements in David Bohm's Physics, The Perennial Philosophy, and Seth*. The Woodbridge Group, 2012 (reissued edition).

John G. Fuller, *The Airmen Who Would Not Die*. Penguin, 1979.

Foster Gamble, Thrive Movement: *http://www.thrivemovement.com/home*

Richard Gerber, *Vibrational Medicine: The #1 Handbook of Subtle-Energy Therapies*. Bear & Company, 3rd edition, 2001.

Nassim Haramein, *Crossing the Event Horizon: Rise to the Equation* (DVD).

_____, Resonance Science Foundation, *https://www.resonancescience.org/*

David R. Hawkins, MD. *Power vs. Force*. Hay House, 2014.

_____, *The Eye of the I: From Which Nothing Is Hidden*. Hay House, 2016.

_____, *I — Reality and Subjectivity*. Hay House, 2014 (reprint edition).

_____, *Truth vs. Falsehood: How to Tell the Difference*. Veritas Publishing, 2005.

_____, *In the World but Not of It* series ("Peace," "Living Spiritually in the Modern World," "Success"). Veritas Publishing (audiobooks).

_____, *The highest Level of Enlightenment: Tap the Database for Total Self-Realization*. Nightingale Conant, 2003 (audiobook).

International Academy of Consciousness (IAC): *https://www.iacworld.org*

Ibrahim Karim, *Back to a Future for Mankind: BioGeometry*. Createspace, 2010.

Ervin Laszlo, *Science and the Akashic Field: An Integral Theory of Everything*. Inner Traditions, 2007 (2nd edition).

Lynne McTaggart, *The Field: The Quest for the Secret Force in the Universe*. Harper Perennial, 2008 (updated edition).

Drunvalo Melchizedek, *The Ancient Secret of the Flower of Life*. Light Technology Publishing, 1999.

Robert A. Monroe, *Journeys Out of the Body*. Broadway Books, 1992 (updated edition).

_____, *Far Journeys*. Harmony, 1987 (reissued edition).

_____, *Ultimate Journey*. Harmony, 1994 (15th printing).

James Oschman, *Energy Medicine in Therapeutics and Human Performance*. Butterworth-Heinemann, 2003.

Walter Russell and Lao Russell, *Home Study Course: Universal Law, Natural Science, and Living Philosophy*. Univ. of Science and Philosophy, 2015 (3rd edition).

Zecharia Sitchin, *Earth Chronicles*. Bear & Company, 2014 (collectors' edition).

Michael Talbot, *The Holographic Universe: The Revolutionary Theory of Reality*. Harper Perennial, 2011 (reprint edition).

Robert Waggoner, *Lucid Dreaming: Gateway to the Inner Self*. Moment Point Press, 2008.

David Wilcock, *https://www.divinecosmos.com*

_____, *The Source Field Investigations: The Hidden Science and Lost Civilizations Behind the 2012 Prophecies*. Dutton, 2012.

Paramahansa Yogananda, *Autobiography of a Yogi*. Self-Realization Fellowship, 1998 (reprint edition).

Arthur M. Young, *The Reflexive Universe: Evolution of Consciousness*. Anodos Foundation, 1999 (revised edition).

_____, *The Geometry of Meaning*. Anodos Foundation, 2003.

Chapter 13: The Mystery of 3-6-9

Bagua: *https://en.wikipedia.org/wiki/Bagua*

BioGeometry pendulums (e.g., BG16 or IKUP) available from *https://biogeometry.ca*, as well as various BioGeometry distributors, such as: *https://www.FMBR.org*, or *https://vesica.org/product-category/vesica-shop/biogeometry/biogeometry-tools-for-the-public/*, or *https://bebodhiinc.com/product-category/student-tools/*, and others.

Eight Trigrams: *https://en.wikipedia.org/wiki/Bagua*

Robert Gilbert, "The Neutral Pendulum": *https://youtu.be/rklULOn8p0w*

Ibrahim Karim, *Back to a Future for Mankind: BioGeometry*. Createspace, 2010.

_____ *BioGeometry Signatures: Harmonizing the Body's Subtle Energy Exchange with the Environment.* Createspace, 2016.

Randy Powell on Symbol of Enlightenment: *https://joedubs.com/vortex-based-mathematics-numerically-conceptualizing-reality*

Marko Rodin on Symbol of Enlightenment: *https://globalbem.com/marko-rodin/*

Nikola Tesla quotation and Nikunj Bangad on AUM: *https://www.quora.com/Why-did-Tesla-say-that-3-6-and-9-was-the-key-to-the-universe*

References: Figures

Figure 1: My first pendulum (a string and a nut), and some spoons turned into pretzels. Source: Jerry Gin

Figure 2: The double-slit experiment. Source: Johannes Kalliauer, Creative Commons BY-SA4.0

Figure 3: Kirlian photo of a dusty miller leaf. Source: Dusty miller leaf by Mark D. Roberts, Creative Commons BY-SA 4.0

Figure 4: Model of a torus. Source: Jerry Gin

Figure 5: Walter Russell's view of creation. Source: Walter Russell, in *In the Wave Lies the Secret of Creation: Containing Scientific paintings and Charts of Walter Russell*, with commentaries by Dr. Timothy A. Binder, University of Science and Philosophy, page 62

Figure 6: The basis of the creation of matter: clockwise centripetal gravitational vortex inward to the center of the two lights, red and blue. Source: Walter Russell, in *In the Wave Lies the Secret of Creation: Containing Scientific paintings and Charts of Walter Russell*, with commentaries by Dr. Timothy A. Binder, University of Science and Philosophy, page 21

Figure 7: The basis of the creation of matter: the cones of the vortex. Source: Walter Russell, *The Universal One*. Volume One, edited by Louise Russell, University of Science and Philosophy, page 153

Figure 8: The basis of the creation of matter: Nature's method of storing energy in mass. Source: Walter Russell, *The Universal One*. Volume One, Edited by Louise Russell, University of Science and Philosophy, page 178

Figure 9: The "Anu"—the basic building block of matter—the spiral motion of the aether. Source: "Ultramicroscopic seeing" of matter: the "ultimate" physical atom. Charles Leadbetter and Annie Besant, *Occult Chemistry: Investigations by Clairvoyant Magnification into the Structure of the Atoms of the Periodic Table and Some Compounds*. (1908) Kessinger Publishing, 2010.

Figure 10: Vector Equilibrium (VE), or cuboctahedron. Source: Drawing by Jerry Gin

Figure 11: Cuboctahedron—Icosahedron—Octahedron. Source: Drawing by Jerry Gin

Figure 12: Isotropic Vector Matrix (IVM). Source: Drawing by Jerry Gin

Figure 13: Homemade pendulum using a string and a nut. Source: Jerry Gin

Figure 14: Pendulum held for dowsing. Source: Walt Woods, *Letter to Robin: A Mini-Course on Pendulum Dowsing*. Walter Woods, 1998 (revised edition).

Figure 15: Directional guide for using a pendulum. Source: Walt Woods, *Letter to Robin: A Mini-Course on Pendulum Dowsing*. Walter Woods, 1998 (revised edition).

Figure 16: Resonance analogy. Source: Jerry Gin, "The Science of BioGeometry," in *Cosmos and History: The Journal of Natural and Social Philosophy*, vol. 11, no. 2, 2015, page 290; originally in Ibrahim Karim's book, *Back to a Future for Mankind: BioGeometry*. I had Ibrahim's permission for use of the figure in my article, *The Science of BioGeometry*.

Figure 17: Pendulums made of salt, flour, water + string. Source: Jerry Gin

Figure 18: Pendulums made of acrylic (top) and wood (bottom). Source: Jerry Gin

Figure 19 (A-D): How to find a pendulum's clockwise-rotation length (personal wavelength) . Source: Jerry Gin

Figure 20: Holding the L-rod, with a counterclockwise rotation. Source: Jerry Gin

Figure 21: Colors found by resonance in a sphere facing the sun and on circle drawn on paper, with compass directions indicated. Source: Jerry Gin, "The Science of BioGeometry," in *Cosmos and History: The Journal of Natural and Social Philosophy*, vol. 11, no. 2, 2015, page 290; originally in Ibrahim Karim's book, *Back to a Future for Mankind: BioGeometry*. I had Ibrahim's permission for use of the figure in my article, *The Science of BioGeometry*.

Figure 22: The male and female polar elements seeking balance. Source: *In the Wave Lies the Secret of Creation: Containing Scientific Paintings and Charts of Walter Russell*, with commentaries by Dr. Timothy A. Binder, University of Science and Philosophy, page 22

Figure 23: Visualizing 3-6-9 in torus / BG3 within torus. Source: Drawing by Jerry Gin

Figure 24: The numbers 3-6-9 and BG3. Source: Drawing by Jerry Gin

Figure 25: 3-6-9 as vertical units. Source: Drawing by Jerry Gin

Figure 26: Yin Yang is part of the vertical cross-section of a torus. Source: Drawing by Jerry Gin

Figure 27: Yin Yang spiral in the torus (view from above). Source: Drawing by Jerry Gin

References: Figures

Figure 28: Harmony from joining CW and CCS spiral. Source: Jerry Gin

Figure 29: 3-6-9 and AUM. Source: Nkunj Bangad, *https://www.quora.com/Why-did-Tesla-say-that-3-6-and-9-was-the-key-to-the-universe*

Figure 30: The Vortex Math structure. Source: *https://joedubs.com/vortex-based-mathematics-numerically-conceptualizing-reality/*

Figure 31: The Vortex Math Structure with connecting lines, producing 3-6-9 and BG3. Source: Drawing by Jerry Gin

Figure 32: The Bagua structure. Source: *https://en.wikipedia.org/wiki/Bagua*

Figure 33: Reiki symbols. Source: Compilation of Reiki symbols from Internet

Figure 34: The Reiki power symbol (has BG3 and 3-6-9). Source: Compilation of Reiki symbols from Internet

Figure 35 (A-C): The L-90 structure and the 3-6-9 lines. Source: Drawings by Jerry Gin. L-90 are sections from Emitter sheets from BioGeometry Courses

Figure 36: Various torus structures (drawn clockwise) containing BG3 except in the center, but the center does have 3-6-9. Source: Drawings by Jerry Gin; images from internet for bagua and power symbol

Acknowledgments

Naomi Rose, my editor, has truly helped clarify the material in this book by getting me to state its concepts in a more understandable form.

I appreciate Jan Walsh's inputs to this book, especially as I was writing and organizing some of Joachim's affirmations.

Yana Mocak had excellent inputs to my early drafts regarding correcting sentence structure.

Rick Skalsky gave me encouragement.

Thanks to Margaret Copeland for her graphics and design, and to Mary Lou Arum for her artwork.

Thanks to my wonderful wife, Peggy, who always supported my efforts in completing this book.

Thanks to Cindy Spring who introduced me to Naomi. Cindy, working with my channeling friend, Regina Ochoa, checked with her deceased friend, Dr. Frances Vaughan, to allow me to use her wonderful channeled poem, "I AM the I AM."

About the Author

Jerry Gin is the chairman and CEO of FMBR (Foundation for Mind-Being Research), a non-profit organization that seeks to advance the consciousness of individuals and organizations to enable us to live in greater harmony with one another, the earth, and the cosmos. His credentials span both science and business, with a PhD in Biochemistry from UC Berkeley, a BS from the University of Arizona, and an MBA from Loyola College. He has held Director positions at Dow Pharmaceuticals and Syva/Syntex. His professional science activities include laboratory medicine, clinical chemistry, pharmaceuticals, ophthalmology, and dentistry. His entrepreneurial activities include founding ChemTrak (developed the first home cholesterol test), Oculex Pharmaceuticals (developed the first intraocular drug delivery), Nuvora (developed products that offer sustained delivery for the mouth), Visionex (ophthalmic diagnostic), and Livionex (dental gel, metal modulation).

Jerry's driving passion for the past 20 years has been exploring the nature of the universe. To this end, his activities have included research, studies in many diverse disciplines, experiential activities in self-exploration, and growth and knowledge through inner knowing. The current book, *The Seeker and The Teacher of Light*, is a culmination of his views as to the nature of the universe, as well as the views of his friend, Joachim Wippich. Jerry's website is *www.jerrygin.com*. He can be reached at *jerry@jerrygin.com*.